SOCIAL EXCLUSION IN THE UK

THE
LIVED
EXPERIENCE

Other books you may be interested in:

Gypsies, Roma and Travellers – A Contemporary Analysis
Declan Henry   ISBN 978-1-915080-04-2

Young Refugees and Asylum Seekers: The Truth About Britain
Declan Henry   ISBN 978-1-913063-97-9

Dilemmas and Decision Making in Social Work
Abbi Jackson   ISBN 978-1-914171-20-8

Social Work and Covid-19: Lessons for Education and Practice
Edited by Denise Turner   ISBN 978-1-913453-61-9

Out of the Shadows: The Role of Social Workers in Disasters
Edited by Angie Bartoli, Maris Stratulis and Rebekah Pierre   ISBN 978-1-915080-07-3

*The Anti-racist Social Worker: Stories of Activism by Social Care
and Allied Health Professionals*
Edited by Tanya Moore and Glory Simango   ISBN 978-1-914171-41-3

To order, or for details of our bulk discounts, please go to our website www.criticalpublishing.com or contact our distributor, Ingram Publisher Services (IPS UK), 10 Thornbury Road, Plymouth PL6 7PP, telephone 01752 202301 or email IPSUK.orders@ingramcontent.com.

CRITICAL
PUBLISHING

SOCIAL EXCLUSION IN THE UK

THE LIVED EXPERIENCE

Edited by Mel Hughes

First published in 2022 by Critical Publishing Ltd

British Library Cataloguing in Publication Data
A CIP record for this book is available from the British Library

ISBN: 978-1-915080-38-7

This book is also available in the following e-book formats:
EPUB ISBN: 978-1-915080-39-4
Adobe e-book ISBN: 978-1-915080-40-0

Cover and text design by Out of House Limited
Project management by Newgen Publishing UK
Printed and bound in Great Britain by 4edge, Essex

Critical Publishing
3 Connaught Road
St Albans
AL3 5RX

www.criticalpublishing.com

Printed on FSC accredited paper

Contents

Acknowledgements

This book is dedicated to all the contributors and supporters whose insight, expertise and willingness to share your stories have led to a textbook which places lived experience expertise at the heart of the narrative on social exclusion, marginalisation and social stigma in the UK.

A special thank you to Peter Atkins, Angela Warren and all the members of the Bournemouth (BU) PIER partnership and to the BU social work team for your lifelong commitment to lived experience expertise.

Power to the people!

Royalties from this book will be donated to the Health Bus Trust. The Health Bus provides a mobile health facility that travels to areas where people sleep rough, providing basic health care, a GP service and access to addiction and mental health support services.

Meet the contributors

Ahed Al Hamwi is a social services community interpreter and co-author of the chapter on being a refugee.

Christine Bondsfield is a survivor of domestic abuse and wishes to share her story and anguish she went through with professionals.

Shannon Cullen is a care leaver, final-year social work student and contributor to the chapter on being in care.

Samantha Dawson is a mother, grandmother and woman living with HIV, who among many things manages an HIV charity.

Orlanda Harvey is a social work lecturer at Bournemouth University with interests in domestic abuse, substance use, reflective practice and leadership, and is also a social worker.

Mel Hughes in associate professor in social work, deputy director of the Research Centre for Seldom Heard Voices and Academic Lead for the PIER (Public Involvement in Education and Research) Partnership at Bournemouth University.

Venus Ip, **Lee Forde**, **Niamh Howlett** and **Jasmine Thomson** are social work degree students at Bournemouth University and contributors to the 'Becoming an activist' chapter.

Dr Sally Lee is Programme Lead of the BA and MA qualifying social work programmes at Bournemouth University and an experienced social worker in adult social care.

Tilia Lenz is a senior lecturer in social work at Bournemouth University and has 15 years of front-line experience in children's social care as a practitioner and manager.

Jay Alex Murray is an out and proud trans man, co-founder of a transgender charity, a volunteer and mentor for other like minds.

Margarete Parrish, PhD, is a senior lecturer in social work at Bournemouth University. Her practice background is in health and mental health settings, where she concentrated on working with survivors of trauma.

Phil is in recovery and a peer mentor and volunteer with the charity We Are With You.

Lisa-Marie Price is of Gypsy heritage and is a student at the University of Worcester.

Rachael Sawers is the community support and volunteer manager at International Care Network, a Bournemouth-based charity supporting refugees, asylum seekers and vulnerable migrants. She has a background in international development and trauma healing.

Hannah Stott is a social work student at Bournemouth University and completed her first substantive placement with the substance use charity We Are With You.

Peter Unwin is a principal lecturer at the University of Worcester and an ally member of the Gypsy, Roma and Traveller Social Work Association.

Richard Williams is senior lecturer in social work at Bournemouth University with extensive experience as a social worker and researcher in education and children's social care.

Myka Wilshire is manager for a drug and alcohol project who has lived experience of being a female in prison.

This book places the expertise of people with lived experiences front and centre of the narrative on social exclusion, marginalisation and social stigma in the UK. By harnessing lived experience expertise, we aim to challenge taken-for-granted norms and assumptions of some of the most marginalised and excluded people in UK society. Throughout the book we present a range of lived experiences alongside a critical commentary of the impact of social stigma, exclusion and marginalisation on people's lives. The contributors to this book chose to be involved for many reasons. They hope that sharing their stories will improve life for themselves, their families and for others experiencing stigma and social exclusion. As a reader of this book, we encourage you to put yourself in the shoes of the people you are reading about. We are keen that you develop insight, understanding and compassion for the most marginalised in our society but that you also take action to challenge it. As well as making connections with people, hearing their stories and showing compassion for their situation, we hope that you will reach out to people in your own community, and use your voice and your platform to challenge structures, policies and practices which sustain social exclusion.

Overview of the book

The book has been co-authored with people with lived experience, social work academics and students who present real-world narratives and lived experiences of being marginalised, excluded or stigmatised within UK society and of taking action to challenge it. Narratives include the lived experience of being a child in care, transgender, HIV positive, a refugee, a parent involved in child protection, a heroin and crack user, Romany Gypsy, and being in prison. There are many other individuals and groups who are systematically marginalised, excluded and stigmatised in the UK. In reading these stories, seeing the impact of social exclusion and stigma, and hearing what fosters inclusion, we encourage you to reflect on the experiences of other individuals and groups too.

Transformative learning

The content of this book is underpinned by transformative learning theory, which was developed by Jack Mezirow in the 1990s. Transformative learning involves questioning and challenging our taken-for-granted assumptions and cultural norms. We often grow up being told, hearing or believing things that we take for granted and assume to be true about different groups within society. Critical reflection and transformative learning involve challenging the basis of our knowledge and assumptions. It encapsulates the notion of perspective transformation or a change to a person's frame of reference to one which is '*more inclusive, differentiating, permeable, critically reflective of assumptions, emotionally capable of change and integrative of experience*' (Mezirow, 2000, p 19). We make meaning of our experiences by drawing on our existing knowledge: previous experiences, what we have learnt from others and our frame of reference or mindset. We only know what we know. Transformative learning occurs when we are open to other viewpoints and when these lead to changes or developments in our thinking and actions.

Mezirow identified ten phases of the transformative learning process, which he suggests occur as we seek to clarify meaning based on new information. The process starts with a disorientating dilemma, ie hearing or seeing something that challenges what we thought we knew. The model takes us through several stages of adjusting to this newfound knowledge:

> » a disorientating dilemma;
> » self-examination with feelings of fear, anger, guilt or shame;
> » a critical assessment of assumptions;
> » recognition of one's discontent and the process of transformation are shared;
> » exploration of options for new roles, relationships and actions;
> » planning a course of action;
> » acquiring knowledge and skills for implementing one's plans;
> » provisional trying of one's roles;
> » building competence and self-confidence in new roles and relationships;
> » a reintegration into one's life on the basis of conditions dictated to by one's new perspective.

(Mezirow, 2003, p 4)

Transformative learning does not have to follow these distinct or linear stages (Cranton, 2002; Merriam and Ntseane, 2008; Merriam and Kim, 2008; Walton, 2010; Hughes, 2012). The ten phases model however can be useful in reflecting on how our thinking can be challenged so we can become more inclusive.

The purpose of this book is to provide a range of 'disorientating dilemmas' which challenge what you thought you knew, including assumptions, preconceptions or views on the socially excluded and stigmatised groups being considered. As you read this book, we encourage you to consider and reflect on your own beliefs and perceptions of different stigmatised and socially excluded individuals and groups and to reflect on whether your views change or develop.

Why this book is needed

Often those who are most affected by economic, social and health inequalities are the least likely to be involved in shaping and informing responses to it. This lack of involvement risks further excluding those who are already marginalised. Systems, policies and practices which fail to take into account a diverse range of lived experiences and are based on a narrow set of cultural norms will inevitably reinforce existing inequalities. The impact of this has been well evidenced in recent discourse regarding Covid-19 inequalities (where some communities were more impacted than others) and Black Lives Matter. Focus on specific experiences and research evidence brought an awareness of inequalities and the extent of the social exclusion and stigmatisation of some groups within UK society to the attention of many in the UK and beyond. When certain communities are not involved in the planning and development of systems, policies and practices, it is inevitable that these won't reflect their needs.

This book seeks to challenge the lack of involvement of seldom-heard groups by:

> » legitimising and prioritising lived experience expertise;
> » challenging taken-for-granted assumptions and cultural norms;
> » fostering critical reflection of our own beliefs and assumptions;
> » drawing on lived experience expertise to inform responses and solutions to social, economic and health inequalities and social exclusion and stigmatisation.

Relevance to social work

The Professional Capabilities Framework (PCF) for social work clearly identifies the need for registered social workers and students to challenge social justice and develop anti-oppressive practice. The need to learn from people with lived experiences is embedded throughout Social Work England's 2021 Standards for Social Work Education. The same applies for registered social workers. Standard 1 of the Professional Standards for social work is to: '*Promote the rights, strengths, and wellbeing of people, families and communities.*' This includes the need for social workers to '*Recognise differences across diverse communities and challenge the impact of disadvantage and discrimination on people and their families and communities'* (standard 1.5) and to *'Promote social justice, helping to confront and resolve issues of inequality and inclusion'* (standard 1.6).

The focus on social justice is also integral to the global definition of social work:

Social work is a practice-based profession and an academic discipline that promotes social change and development, social cohesion, and the empowerment and liberation of people. Principles of social justice, human rights, collective responsibility and respect for diversities are central to social work. Underpinned by theories of social work, social sciences, human-ities and indigenous knowledges, social work engages people and structures to address life challenges and enhance wellbeing. The above definition may be amplified at national and/or regional levels.

(International Federation of Social Workers, 2014)

As social workers, it is not enough to be reactive or respond to a presenting need in our practice. The national standards and global definition clearly outline our respon-sibilities to promote social change and development, social cohesion, empowerment and liberation of people.

Relevance to a broader audience

Throughout the book we will identify the causes and consequences of social exclusion and stigma, considering how this develops and is sustained in UK society. We include a number of reflective activities and tasks to enable you to reflect on this in the context of your own life and experiences. The book is relevant not only to social workers but to health and social care students and practitioners, social scientists, educators and all people seeking to promote social inclusion.

How this book promotes critical thinking.

Throughout the book we have included text boxes and activities to promote critical thinking.

We invite you, as the reader, to engage in the narratives and explore your own preconceptions. You will be encouraged to go beyond the acknowledgement of preconceptions and judgements by questioning why and how these views developed and what impact they have had on how you view other people.

How people have participated

Contributors to this book have been supported to develop their chapter in whichever way they chose. This was to ensure that everyone could fully participate as an equal partner in the book. Options included writing the chapter independently; being paired with a mentor to plan and write the chapter; and contributing verbally with the chapter being constructed from audio recordings. When thinking about social exclusion, there is often a focus on equality (treating everyone the same) but in this book we promote equity (treating everyone fairly). We are all different; we have different starting points and different needs. Treating everyone the same fails to acknowledge or celebrate difference. Treating everyone equitably has enabled people to contribute their expertise in a range of ways and for us to include a range of seldom-heard voices.

What this book covers

Chapters 1 and 2 provide a theoretical framework for this book. Key theories and concepts are explained and explored in relation to the UK context. Themes emerging from these chapters are applied and considered throughout the book in relation to different lived experiences.

Chapter 1: 'Understanding social exclusion' by Sally Lee

This chapter draws on definitions of social exclusion, marginalisation, social inclusion and integration. It considers evidence of social exclusion in the UK and the barriers preventing some citizens from full and active participation in society. Specifically, it focuses on what social exclusion is, why it happens and what impact it has on individuals and society. You will be encouraged, through the use of reflective activities, to identify your own experiences of social exclusion and inclusion and consider these in relation to others.

Chapter 2: 'Understanding stigma' by Margarete Parrish

Building on the themes identified in Chapter 1, this chapter draws on key theories to help build your understanding of stigma. The concept of stigma is explored in relation to attribution theory, role theory and social stigma theory. Types of stigma are identified and the reasons why and how we make judgements about others are explored.

Specifically, this chapter covers what social stigma is, why it happens and what impact it has. You will be encouraged, through the use of reflective activities, to identify your own experiences of social stigma and consider these in relation to others.

Chapters 3 to 10

Chapters 3 to 10 are written by people who have experienced stigma and social exclusion, with the support of social work academics and students. Each chapter focuses on personal accounts and reflective narratives of their lived and living experiences. Each contributor was asked to consider:

- » their life and experiences;
- » how others see them, covering commonly held views, preconceptions and stereotypes;
- » impact of social stigma and/or social exclusion;
- » what promotes social inclusion.

Text boxes have been incorporated throughout each chapter to provide formal knowledge (legislation, policy, research, wider literature and evidence) in the form of bitesize quotes, statistics or short explanations to underpin the author's experience. For example, if a contributor discusses their experience of drug taking as a teenager, a text box has been used to identify statistics which demonstrate the prevalence of this in England or the UK. This is to enable you as the reader to consider the person's lived experience in the wider context. Reflective activities have also been incorporated into each chapter, enabling you to engage in transformative learning and reflect on your own views and perceptions. Reflective activities have been co-created with the chapter contributors.

Chapters 3 to 10 are as follows.

- » 'Being in care.'
- » 'Being transgender.'
- » 'Being a heroin and crack user.'
- » 'Being a refugee.'
- » 'Being a parent in the child protection system.'
- » 'Being HIV positive.'
- » 'Being in prison.'
- » 'Being a Gypsy.'

Chapter 11: 'Becoming an activist' by Mel Hughes

This chapter builds on the themes identified in the personal narrative chapters and explores what you, as the reader, can do to reduce social stigma and promote social inclusion. Specific emphasis is placed on social justice models of involvement where full active participation in society is recognised as a right. Consideration will be given to what we can all do to create a more inclusive society. The chapter showcases a number of case studies by social work students engaging in social activism to show what can be achieved.

Conclusion

The conclusion draws the book to a close with an overview of what the book has sought to achieve and what your learning from it might be. It draws out some key themes from the different chapters and considers the impact (positive and negative) of different experiences. It emphasises that each experience is unique to the person who shared it and encourages you to consider the wide range of experiences and expertise that you could draw on so as not to assume that this applies to everyone. This section provides suggestions for further work in the future.

Chapter structure

Each chapter incorporates the following so you can continue to build on your learning and explore topics that you are keen to develop further.

- » Text boxes incorporating formal knowledge (legislation, policy, research, wider literature and evidence) in the form of bitesize quotes, statistics or short explanations to underpin the author's experience.

- » Reflective activities in the form of critical questions, points to consider and tasks which foster criticality and transformative learning.

- » Recommended further reading/viewing. These cover academic sources and signposting to resources including documentaries, films, TED talks, YouTube clips, websites and campaigns which provide further insight into lived experiences and examples of action.

References

British Association of Social Workers (BASW) (2018) Professional Capabilities Framework for Social Work. [online] Available at: www.basw.co.uk/social-work-training/professional-capabilities-framework-pcf (accessed 8 August 2022).

Cranton, P (2002) Teaching for Transformation. *New Directions for Adult and Continuing Education*, 93: 63–72.

Hughes, M (2012) *Is Social Work Education Life Changing? A Unitary Appreciative Inquiry into the Impact of Social Work Education on a Person's Beliefs, Values and Behaviour*. PhD thesis, Bournemouth University.

International Federation of Social Workers (IFFSW) (2014) Global Definition of Social Work. [online] Available at: www.ifsw.org/what-is-social-work/global-definition-of-social-work (accessed 8 August 2022).

Merriam, S B and Kim, Y S (2008) Non-Western Perspectives in Learning and Knowing. *New Directions for Adult and Continuing Education*, 119: 71–81.

Merriam, S B and Ntseane, G (2008) Transformative Learning in Botswana: How Culture Shapes the Process. *Adult Education Quarterly*, 58(3): 183–97.

Mezirow, J (2000) *Learning as Transformation: Critical Perspectives on a Theory in Progress*. San Francisco: Jossey-Bass.

Mezirow, J (2003) *Epistemology of Transformative Learning*. [online] Available at: https://skat.ihmc.us/rid=1LW06CB3L-1R1W965-1Z5Z/Copy%20of%20Mezirow_EpistemologyTLC.pdf (accessed 8 August 2022).

Social Work England (2019) Professional Standards. [online] Available at: www.socialworkengland.org.uk/standards/professional-standards (accessed 8 August 2022).

Social Work England (2021) Standards for Social Work Education. [online] Available at: www.socialworkengland.org.uk/standards/education-and-training-standards (accessed 8 August 2022).

Walton, J D (2010) Examining a Transformative Approach to Communication Education: A Teacher-Research Study. *College Student Journal*, 44(1), 157–77.

Chapter 1 | Understanding social exclusion

Sally Lee

Chapter objectives

This chapter will help readers:

» understand the meaning of social exclusion and key related terms;

» gain insight into the socio-political and economic factors within the current context of life in the UK which give rise to social exclusion;

» understand individual and social factors leading to social exclusion;

» understand the complexity of social exclusion, which is both an outcome and consequence of disadvantage;

» to use reflective exercises to identify their own experiences of social exclusion and inclusion and consider these in relation to others.

Note to reader: Reading about social exclusion and its causes and impacts on everyday life requires you to engage with some uncomfortable information about contemporary life in the UK. The author of this chapter hopes that any discomfort you feel provokes curiosity about the society in which you live and encourages you to seek more information, learn more about the forms and processes of exclusion and think about how you can contribute to an inclusive society.

This chapter explores the meaning of social exclusion and social inclusion and integration to provide insight into how and why some people in UK society experience social exclusion. The chapter considers evidence of social exclusion in the UK and the barriers preventing some citizens from full and active participation in society. The discussion draws on knowledge about contemporary socio-political and economic conditions which give rise to, and perpetuate, social exclusion and considers how all citizens lose out when a society is characterised by the social exclusion of some of its members.

The chapter uses activities to provide engaging routes for readers to reflect on personal experiences of social exclusion and inclusion and consider these in relation to the experience of other citizens.

What is social exclusion?

Although there is no universally agreed definition of the term *social exclusion*, it is used to signify the ways in which experience of different forms of disadvantage cut people off from 'normal' life (Backwith, 2015, p 32). The result of being cut off from participation in the social, economic and political networks which a society sees as constituting part of a normal life is exclusion from the (often assumed or taken-for-granted), advantages, knowledge and activities of citizenship. This means the information, protections, rights and responsibilities associated with citizenship are compromised and consequently the ties that create social cohesion are eroded. As such, the impact of social exclusion is experienced at the micro level of individuals and families and at the macro level of whole societies (Pickett and Wilkinson, 2010).

Use of the term social exclusion to examine, explain, understand and describe observed lived experience of disadvantage emerged from France in the 1970s (UN, 2016). At that time in France, there was a perception that social cohesion was breaking down after civil unrest in the late 1960s and this perception led to the introduction of policy initiatives aimed at facilitating social inclusion. This approach was adopted across the European Union, resulting in the focus of social policy moving from economic poverty to a wider, multi-factored understanding of disadvantage and exclusion. In the UK the Labour government (1997–2010) promoted the notion of social exclusion and established the Social Exclusion Unit, which aimed to take a multi-dimensional approach to addressing the complex impacts of social exclusion. Since that time, use of the term in UK social policy has declined and discourse has changed to focus on specific groups, for example 'troubled families' (Hayden and Jenkins, 2014).

While the concept of social exclusion can be critiqued as vague because it attempts to capture a broad range of disadvantage (Pierson and Thomas, 2013), and is contested (for example, Murray [1996] argues that social exclusion is caused by people excluding themselves through their own actions), it is a concept that reflects the complexity of the lived experience of disadvantage. It moves understanding beyond the historic focus on economic poverty to include other forms of poverty, for example of information, access, opportunity and participation in the rights and benefits of society. Engaging with the broader notion of social exclusion leads to consideration of the nature of disadvantage which drives exclusion and how and why the drivers of exclusion occur. This includes examination of the social relations and processes by which people become excluded from wider society.

Disadvantage is an enduring feature of society. Social policy over many decades has aimed to tackle disadvantage in support of societal progress (which is generally measured by gross domestic product or GDP), such as through provision of education because an educated workforce is good for the individual, their family and the economy (Pickett and Wilkinson, 2010). Historically, disadvantaged people might be supported through charity and the church. The earliest example of social policy in the UK is the Poor Law 1601, amended in 1824, which established forms of poor relief, including workhouses. Such relief assessed eligibility and made strict judgements on who was deserving of support (such as widows and orphans who were seen as blameless) and who was undeserving (such as single mothers and substance users who were seen as causing their own misfortune). These founding principles of deserving and undeserving are evident in contemporary Britain in public discourse and social policy (Horner, 2019), as evidenced in the stories contained in this book.

The discourse of deserving or undeserving is closely aligned to notions about the causes of disadvantage and ideas about personal responsibility, which are reflected in the values and views of different political parties and the social policy they implement (Levitas et al, 2007). Are individuals to blame for their situation or are there wider societal causes? Disadvantage and consequent social exclusion are viewed by some as a matter of personal and moral responsibility; that while an individual cannot be responsible for their birth circumstances, they are responsible for improving their own lives (Murray, 1996). Other thinkers appreciate that disadvantage has profound effects on child and adult development and impacts across a lifetime (UN, 2016).

Research exploring adverse childhood experiences (ACEs) illustrates the lifelong physiological and psychological effects of kinds of life experiences. ACEs, especially when experienced at a young age, alter brain development, cause trauma and can lead to the sorts of behaviours associated with the discourse of 'undeserving', for example substance use or unhealthy lifestyles (Moustafa et al, 2018; Boppre and Boyer, 2021). For many people who experience disadvantage and social exclusion, improving life, for example by controlling use of substances or gaining stable and well-paid employ-ment, may require resources they do not have access to, be it transport, a home, or protective family or social networks. This means for many socially excluded people whose lives and futures have been characterised by disadvantage, being instructed to 'get clean' or 'get a job' is not as simple as such statements suggest.

Sociological research also indicates how the structures of social organisation which determine status, influence and power (for example, social stratification in relation to class) can reinforce social advantage and disadvantage (Llewellyn et al, 2014). The con-cept of social capital (Bourdieu, 1986; Coleman, 1988; Putnam, 1995) illustrates this point and offers a helpful way to think about how forms of advantage, including social resources and goods, facilitate social inclusion. The concept of social capital introduces ideas about different forms of capital citizens may have through the circumstances of their birth, their community and which accrue during their lives. Social capital includes economic wealth but also the advantages of social networks and cultural capital, including experience of culture, arts and education and symbolic capital such as status, respect and reputation. Possession of these forms of social capital enables individuals, communities and societies to participate in the *'networks, norms and social trust that facilitate coordination and cooperation for mutual benefit'* (Putnam, 1995, p 67). Putnam (1995) also discusses how social or civic networks (which can range from small scale and local such as sports clubs to large-scale party-political affiliations) are the foundation of social capital and create the bonds of social cohesion through reinforcement of norms, such as what is considered to be acceptable behaviour. The social advantages gained through the possession of social capital can be both obvious and easily measurable, such as inherited wealth or social connections (who you went to school with, for example) and more subtle, therefore not clearly measurable, such as family support. Generally, in the UK it is assumed that parents support their children often into adulthood throughout their lives. This might be by helping them develop numeracy and literacy skills, or helping them learn to drive, or maybe even helping them with a deposit to buy a home. However, for many citizens with little or no social capital, any of these examples and many, many more assumptions about what is 'normal' are false. An example of policy based on this assumption is the minimum wage. Lower rates are set for those aged under 18, 18–20, 20–24 and over 25 (Gov.UK, 2021a).

Definitions of social exclusion, social inclusion and social integration.

Social exclusion

As has been discussed, there is no universally agreed definition of social exclusion. However, the range of definitions do share common elements: firstly, that the causes and consequences of social exclusion are complex and multi-dimensional; and secondly, that it creates deep and long-lasting problems which can pass from generation to generation (Social Exclusion Unit, 2004).

Definitions also feature, but give different degrees of priority to, the following areas of focus:

- » *who* is at risk of exclusion;
- » *from what* people are excluded;

» the *problems associated* with social exclusion;

» the *processes driving* exclusion.

(UN, 2016)

The emphasis given to each of the above in any definition reflects the priority of the definer and gives direction to subsequent social policy. For example, if the definition being utilised focuses on *who* is at risk of exclusion, such as young people not in education or training, the resulting policy is likely to focus on that sort of individual or group (Powell, 2021) and may not address any underlying or structural level matters. However, a definition focused on the *processes driving* exclusion, such as financial poverty, may respond to low wages (Gov.UK, 2021a). This point is important as it provides insight into the changing use of the term social exclusion as social discourse moves between focusing on collective responses to disadvantage to more individualised perspectives (Pierson, 2016).

Academics such as Pierson (2016) draw on sociological theory to understand the components of social exclusion of which poverty and low income are fundamental, while other factors such as lack of access to employment, thin or non-existent social support and networks, exclusion from services and the local area or neighbourhood are also important.

Khan et al (2015) identify different forms of social exclusion (which echo forms of social capital involved in social inclusion and are discussed later in this chapter) that prevent individuals or groups from full participation in social, economic and political life and from asserting their rights.

» Political exclusion resulting from denial of, or disengagement from, civic activities such as voting.

» Economic exclusion resulting from poverty and low incomes.

» Social exclusion resulting from weak or non-existent social networks.

» Cultural exclusion resulting from the absence of respect for diverse values, norms and ways of living.

All of the above elements, features, components and forms of social exclusion may be experienced separately or in combination; however, most people experiencing social exclusion will be living with a range of disadvantages and their consequences. The term *deep exclusion* (Levitas et al, 2007, p 9) describes when exclusion is experienced across more than one area of disadvantage, resulting in severe negative consequences for quality of life, well-being and future life chances.

In addition to looking at social exclusion, it may be helpful to consider what social inclusion and social integration are.

Social inclusion

Social inclusion concerns participation in, and benefitting from, the rights and benefits of citizenship, such as access to services, education, employment and good housing. But inclusion also concerns the less tangible aspects of citizenship, including social acceptance, having relationships of choice and participation in civic activities. Experiencing social exclusion is detrimental to health and well-being, and therefore social inclusion is key to mental and physical health (Pierson, 2016). Social policy promotes social inclusion through policies that improve *'the participation in society of people who are disadvantaged on the basis of age, sex, disability, race, ethnicity, origin, religion, or economic or other status, through enhanced opportunities, access to resources, voice and respect for rights'* (UN, 2016, p 20). This means that social inclusion involves actions to remove barriers to participation and actions to enable participation. Many of these are explored in this book from the lived experience perspective.

Social integration

Social integration turns social inclusion into action through implementation of strategies of inclusion which recognise and value diversity. Such strategies promote retention of cultural identity and see value in difference. This means the social relations and structures which form society actively integrating diverse needs, methods of communication, culture and other forms of diversity into how they work. Pierson and Thomas (2013) state that integration requires ethnic hierarchies to be eradicated, opportunity to be equally distributed, and all groups within society to be encouraged to participate in and contribute to all aspects of society. Evidence of the persistence of racist attitudes in the UK is revealed in events which grab headlines, for example the racist abuse so often faced by Black footballers (Kopczyk and Walker-Khan, 2021), but also through personal disclosures of daily micro aggressions.

Pierson and Thomas (2013) suggest that full integration may be more of an aspiration than a reality and social policy is required to create the environment where integration is possible. In England, Scotland and Wales the Equality Act 2010 has promoted the goal of integration. Anti-discrimination is an approach to policy and practice which consciously seeks to challenge the discrimination marginalised people and groups experience and is therefore a way of facilitating social integration.

Barriers preventing citizens from full and active participation in society

This chapter has identified the complex, multi-dimensional nature of social exclusion and this complexity is reflected in the barriers some people experience to their participation in society. The barriers discussed in this section are largely rooted in economic disadvantage. However, overcoming barriers is more complicated than simply having money or resources; barriers are created and maintained by stigma, as discussed later in Chapter 2, lack of insight into the lived experience of social exclusion and the processes of discrimination embedded in personal, cultural and structural attitudes, beliefs and discourse.

Looking at the processes which create and maintain barriers, the Social Exclusion Taskforce (Cabinet Office, 2009) offers a helpful summary of the sorts of interwoven disadvantages that create barriers to full and active participation when experienced by individuals and communities:

- » discrimination;
- » poor housing;
- » low incomes;
- » high crime;
- » family breakdown;
- » unemployment.

This is not an exhaustive list of disadvantages (for example, it does not include health, digital or education inequalities), but it does suggest the sort of disadvantages that are part of the cycle of cause and effect that characterises social exclusion. This cycle means that disadvantages, such as those listed above, are both outcomes and drivers of social exclusion; for example, unemployment may be an outcome of discrimination and a driver of low income or poverty. This should not be read as a suggestion that there is necessarily a linear progression of disadvantage but rather that causes and consequences are woven together so that disadvantage is both something to be overcome and may be the barrier to accessing solutions. It is important to recognise the interwoven and cyclical processes which create barriers to inclusion because effective intervention in the social exclusion cycle requires strategies of change at multiple levels. Specifically, this means interventions at the individual level to improve personal outcomes, at the community level to improve outcomes for whole groups, and at the societal level to ensure social policy, institutions and structures focus on creating the sort of environment in which the causes and consequences of disadvantage are acknowledged and addressed.

An example of UK social policy which acknowledges, and potentially addresses, the impact of disadvantage is the levelling up agenda (Gov.UK, 2021b) overseen by the new Department for Levelling Up, Housing and Communities. This agenda is in response to long-term economic deprivation, underfunding of public services and underinvestment in the private sector in specific geographic locations that has led to poor outcomes from housing to health to education over generations. It intends to feature a series of policies designed to improve personal and community outcomes and Neil O'Brien, MP and levelling up adviser states: *'It's absolutely crucial that we bring opportunity to every single part of the UK by making sure our spending, tax, investment and regeneration priorities bring about meaningful change'* (Gov.UK, 2021d). Critics suggest that this agenda follows earlier, similar strategies which have had little impact, for example the Northern Powerhouse agenda (Gov.UK, 2021c), and will require significant and long-term financial and political commitment to be effective.

Barriers to social inclusion

As has been discussed, barriers to social inclusion relate to social disadvantage and this section of the chapter focuses on examples of specific forms of disadvantage, specifically those related to discrimination, in order to understand what sorts of barriers exist in the UK and how they operate. While this discussion focuses on discrimination, the general points can be applied to other forms of disadvantage.

Discrimination

In relation to social exclusion, discrimination refers to unfair, unequal or prejudicial treatment of or behaviour towards individuals or groups of people who tend to be relatively powerless within their society, for example older people or minority populations. In Great Britain (England, Wales and Scotland) the Equality Act 2010 makes it unlawful to discriminate on the grounds of age, gender reassignment, being married or in a civil partnership, being pregnant or on maternity leave, disability, race including colour, nationality, ethnic or national origin, religion or belief, sex, and sexual orientation, which are termed protected characteristics (for further information go to www.gov.uk/discrimination-your-rights). However, discrimination remains evident in the UK and continues to be a significant barrier to social inclusion (Thompson, 2021). Discrimination can be experienced directly through unfair treatment and indirectly through the implementation of rules or arrangements that apply to everyone but put those with particular characteristics at a disadvantage. Harassment such as unwanted behaviour and victimisation are also forms of discrimination which create barriers to participation.

Thompson (2021) breaks down a generalised understanding of discrimination into specific processes which identify how discrimination occurs. These processes are often reinforced by dominant discourses about people and places that are communicated through social policy and the media.

Stereotyping: the over-simplified, biased and inflexible conception of an individual or social group, for example, Gypsy, Romany and Travellers being seen as a homogenous group who disregard property and the law.

Marginalisation: people are pushed into the margins of society and excluded from the mainstream. For example, people sleeping rough who are excluded from some rights of citizenship such as voting.

Invisibilisation: how some groups of people are not represented in language and the media or are presented as being associated with low status and powerless. For example, people living in poverty despite being employed and who may be ignored by social policy.

Dehumanisation: treating people as objects, diagnoses, categories, irritants, while disregarding their personhood, needs and feelings. For example, hospital patients requiring care services (which are often unavailable) for safe discharge being termed *bed blockers* and treated as a problem or burden to be managed.

Infantilisation: treating adults as 'child like', which is disempowering and a denial of rights and citizenship. For example, learning disabled people who are treated in ways which deny their right to sexual relationships of their choice.

Welfareism: regarding certain individuals or groups as necessarily dependent on welfare services by the virtue of their membership of such groups. For example, whole housing estates in areas of economic deprivation being portrayed as dependent on public services and welfare benefits.

Medicalisation: ascribing the status of 'ill' to someone can make them 'invalid', as well as subject to the welfarism noted above. For example, disabled people whose lives can be portrayed as tragic, or subject to medical intervention and ultimately to be 'cured' rather than being part of human diversity.

Trivialisation: where something important, such as the movement towards gender equality, is made to seem trivial (burning bras, for example).

These processes of discrimination relate to the later discussion in Chapter 2 regarding psychological theories of exclusion; the processes also demonstrate how notions of stigma and labelling are put into action. Thompson (2021) provides a helpful model to understand how discrimination occurs across personal, cultural and structural levels of society, with the levels interacting with and informing each other. The PCS analysis model illustrates how discrimination seeps into personal attitudes and psychological perspectives through socialisation and is embedded in cultural norms and societal institutions and structures. For example, discourse and policy around the promotion of paid employment is presented as a solution to diverse individual and social problems, including poverty.

Thompson argues that critical examination of the taken-for-granted norms of society, including the socio-political and economic policies that shape the social environment, is necessary for social exclusion to be addressed. Without such examination, discrimination is reinforced with consequences for individuals and communities: at its most extreme, discrimination leads to violence, for example hate crimes perpetrated against individuals or groups because of a characteristic or perceived difference (see the Stop Hate Crime campaign at www.stophateuk.org).

What impact does social exclusion have on individuals and society?

Social exclusion is an important lens through which to understand the impact forms of disadvantage have on individuals and communities. Human development, health and well-being are negatively impacted by exclusion from the social conditions, experiences and relationships required for a good quality of life (Pierson, 2016). Healthy development and sustained health and well-being requires human needs to be met. Probably the most well-known presentation of human needs is Maslow's (1943) hierarchy of needs, which builds from the base of essential *physiological or biological needs* for sustaining life, such as food, drink, warmth and sleep, through the need for *safety* such as physical safety, law and order, social stability and job security, to *social belonging* where humans give and receive love, belonging to a family, group or nation, moving on to the need for *esteem* of the self and others and then on to the higher-level needs for *cognitive engagement, aesthetic needs* and ultimately the need for *self-actualisation* and self-fulfilment. Maslow's hierarchy of needs is subject to debate; however, what is important to understand in relation to social exclusion is that humans have needs that range from the basics essential to survival to higher-level needs which are part of what makes a good quality of life. Living with disadvantage cuts people off from opportunities to meet a range of human needs. By reading this book, readers will gain insight into the lived experience of disadvantage but also how this can be addressed.

Returning to the work of Pickett and Wilkinson (2010), the impact of disadvantage, inequality and consequent social exclusion of some populations is felt across society, for example in terms of social cohesion, trust and well-being. Their research suggests that addressing the causes and consequences of social exclusion is important not only for the circumstances of individuals but is key to social progress.

Evidence of social exclusion in the UK

The experience of social exclusion is closely related to inequality, which concerns the unequal distribution of the socio-economic benefits associated with living within a society (Warwick-Booth, 2018). Inequality, like the social disadvantages discussed above, is both a cause and consequence of social exclusion because, for those at the bottom end of the inequality scale, it negatively impacts on their ability to participate in 'normal' life, to refer to the phrase used earlier in the chapter. Pickett and Wilkinson (2010) identify the ways inequality within a society affects the quality of life of citizens, including those experiencing forms of disadvantage as well as wider society. Their ongoing work through the Equality Trust (www.equalitytrust.org.uk) argues that addressing inequality is an essential part of a socially inclusive and fair society.

In the UK there is evidence of significant inequality in how, and to whom, the advantages associated with living in a modern society are distributed. These advantages include participation in and access to wealth and good incomes, education, housing and health. Unequal distribution of advantage impacts on the experience of social inclusion across the whole life course of individuals and their families, and it is largely determined by socio-economic policy, which is in itself an expression of the values of the policy makers. Since the 1980s, economic policy in the UK has promoted neo-liberal views which are characterised by the championing of the notion of individual consumers, along with deregulation, the privatisation and marketisation of public services and 'trickle-down' economics. Critics of neo-liberalism point out that the rise of inequality during the last 40 years, in which wealth (and other forms of social capital such as influence and status) has accumulated in the hands of the minority while the majority have lost out, is an inevitable outcome of implementing neo-liberal economic policies (Fenton, 2016). The austerity agenda initiated in 2010 by the Conservative and Liberal Democrat coalition government reflected neo-liberal priorities in its emphasis on 'small' government and consequent cuts to budgets for public services on which poorer members of society rely more than better-off citizens

(Fenton, 2016). The rise of inequality in the UK demonstrates the effective devaluing and exclusion of some populations, for example people who are economically inactive due to poverty, ill health, age or disability and are insufficiently supported by welfare benefits or care services to enable their social inclusion (Alston, 2019). This point can be illustrated by considering three examples of inequality in the UK: economic, health and housing (but could be applied to other experiences of social exclusion such as inequality of education).

Economic inequality: low income and poverty

Poverty in the UK means that individuals and families have to make choices every day about how to pay for essentials such as housing, heating, food and clothing. Poverty means facing insecurity and having to make impossible decisions about money (Backwith, 2015). Living with such insecurity creates chronic stress, which impacts on individuals' and communities' physical and psychological health, relationships, community connections and connection to a hopeful future (Lansley and Mack, 2015). Poverty is at the heart of multiple and enduring social problems, including social exclusion, because poverty means facing marginalisation and even discrimination because of financial circumstances. The chronic negative impacts lead to the types of problems that deprive people of the chance to play a full part in society (Shildrick and Rucell, 2015).

Evidence of poverty in contemporary UK was highlighted by the UN report in 2019 (Alston, 2019) and has since been further evidenced by, for example, the significant rise in the use of food banks (Trussell Trust, 2021). Food poverty has been highlighted in high-profile campaigns by popular figures such as the footballer Marcus Rashford (see https://endchildfoodpoverty.org).

Health inequality

Social determinants have profound impacts on health, meaning that the conditions in which people live are a significant part of physical and mental health (Siegel et al, 2020). In 2010, Professor Sir Michael Marmot undertook a review of the significant health inequalities in the UK. Marmot (2010) concluded that reducing those inequalities required action in the following six policy areas.

» Give every child the best start in life.

» Enable all children, young people and adults to maximise their capabilities and have control over their lives.

» Create fair employment and good work for all.

» Ensure a healthy standard of living for all.

» Create and develop healthy and sustainable places and communities.

» Strengthen the role and impact of ill-health prevention.

In 2020, Marmot revisited the original review to investigate any changes and concluded that health inequalities have actually widened since 2010. He states that when the Covid-19 pandemic occurred those most vulnerable to pre-existing health inequalities were most vulnerable to the virus. Preventable conditions associated with inequality, including obesity and Type 2 diabetes, are major risk factors for Covid-19 and people who have been worst affected by the virus are generally those who had worse health outcomes before the pandemic, including:

» people working in lower-paid professions;

» people from ethnic minority backgrounds;

» people living in poorer areas.

These findings relate health outcomes to inequality, which reflects the causes and consequences of social exclusion, specifically disadvantage resulting from low income and poverty, discrimination and marginalisation.

Housing inequality

The cost of housing in the UK has increased significantly over recent decades (ONS, 2021). This means citizens are spending a higher proportion of their income on housing. This reduction in affordable housing impacts on people living on low incomes or in poverty the most, a finding evidenced by research from the Department for Work and Pensions (2021), which found that the proportion of the poorest fifth of the UK population who spend more than a third of their income on housing costs has risen and private renters are more likely to spend more than a third of their income on housing. This drain on income leads to instability and stress on individuals and families who struggle to meet other needs, such as maintaining a healthy diet, children being appropriately clothed for school attendance, adequate heating and participation in social events.

Homelessness is perhaps the most obvious example of both social exclusion and inequality; firstly, social exclusion because homelessness can lead to (and be the result of) instability, trauma, disconnection and poverty and secondly, inequality because of the extremes of housing in the UK from a tent pitched in a street to multi-million-pound properties.

There is a powerful negative discourse associated with homelessness, by which people often mean rough sleepers (when the definition of homelessness also extends to people who are sofa surfing, sleeping in their vehicle, staying at a night shelter or hostel and squatting among others; Shelter, 2021). This discourse blames the person and suggests that homeless people are in that situation through choice or because of substance use and they need to 'get clean' and 'get a job' (No Fixed Address, 2017). It is a discourse of blame that does not acknowledge the damaging impacts and causes of homelessness or other forms of social exclusion, including physical and mental health; disability; substance use; trauma; domestic violence; migration; people coping with discrimination on the basis of race, sexual orientation, and gender identity or expression; and the impacts of poverty. To understand and intervene with people experiencing homelessness, it is necessary to understand that the preceding issues affect people, and how these intersect with systemic barriers (Siegel et al, 2020).

The Housing Act 1996 (amended by the Homelessness Act 2002 and the Homelessness Reduction Act 2017) provides the legal framework of homelessness and sets out who is eligible for support with housing. Anyone who is homeless or threatened with homelessness is entitled to advice and assistance from the housing authority and if someone is homeless and has a priority need they must be provided with accommodation; priority need categories include families with dependent children, vulnerability due to physical or mental health needs, disability, age, and if someone has left their property due to violence or the threat of violence. Housing provision even for people in priority need categories can be poor quality and negatively impact on health and well-being, for example overcrowded and poor-condition housing. Those who do not fit into the categories of priority need may become part of the widespread and hidden population of homelessness people who, for example, 'sofa surf' and also experience social exclusion.

Reflective activity

The notion of home is important to our health and well-being. But where we live and where we call home may be different and home often relates to people rather than accommodation itself.

Take time out to consciously look around what/where you call home. What does your home mean to you?

Here is what others have said about their home:

'*The cornerstone of our universe*' (a resettled asylum seeker)

'*Home means my mother's blood sprayed across the walls*' (a victim of domestic abuse)

'*Home means three walls...*' (a rough sleeper)

Home is not something to be taken for granted – can you reflect on this point as you read the accounts of lived experience in this book?

Conclusion

This chapter has discussed the complex, multi-faceted nature of social exclusion and how the barriers to participation are both causes and consequences of exclusion. The chapter has also highlighted the significant and long-lasting detrimental effects of disadvantage and inequality to the meeting of human needs, and their consequent impacts on human development, health and well-being. These drivers of social exclusion have been discussed as phenomena resulting from value being assigned to certain individuals and groups of people over others and expressed through social and economic policy. This book now moves on to explore the impact of social exclusion on a wide range of individuals, demonstrating the relevance of this topic to anyone interested in a society which values inclusion, health and well-being.

References

Alston, P (2019) *Report of the Special Rapporteur on Extreme Poverty and Human Rights on His Visit to the United Kingdom of Great Britain and Northern Ireland. United Nations General Assembly.* [online] Available at: https://undocs.org/A/HRC/41/39/Add.1 (accessed 8 August 2022).

Backwith, D (2015) *Social Work, Poverty and Social Exclusion.* Maidenhead: Open University Press.

Boppre, B and Boyer, C (2021) 'The Traps Started During My Childhood': The Role of Substance Abuse in Women's Responses to Adverse Childhood Experiences (ACEs). *Journal of Aggression, Maltreatment & Trauma,* 30(4), 429–49.

Bourdieu, P (1986) The Forms of Capital. In Richardson, J (ed) *Handbook of Theory and Research for the Sociology of Education* (pp 241–58). New York: Greenwood Press.

Cabinet Office (2009) What Do We Mean by Social Exclusion? [online] Available at: http://webarchive.natio nalarchives.gov.uk/20090114000528/http://cabinetoffice.gov.uk/social_exclusion_task_force/context. aspx (accessed 8 August 2022).

Coleman, J (1988) Social Capital in the Creation of Human Capital. *American Journal of Sociology,* 94: S96–120.

Department of Work and Pensions (2021) Households Below Average Income, 1994/95–2019/20. [Data collection]. 15th Edition. UK Data Service. SN: 5828. http://doi.org/10.5255/UKDA-SN-5828-13

Equality Act 2010 [online] Available at: www.legislation.gov.uk/ukpga/2010/15/contents (accessed 8 August 2022).

Fenton, J (2016) *Values in Social Work*. London: Palgrave.

Gov.UK (2021a) National Minimum Wage and National Living Wage Rates. [online] Available at: www.gov.uk/national-minimum-wage-rates (accessed 8 August 2022).

Gov.UK (2021b) Levelling Up Agenda. Department for Levelling Up, Housing & Communities. [online] Available at: www.gov.uk/government/organisations/department-for-levelling-up-housing-and-communities (accessed 8 August 2022).

Gov.UK (2021c) Industrial Strategy: Working Together to Build the Northern Powerhouse. [online] Available at: https://northernpowerhouse.gov.uk (accessed 8 August 2022).

Gov.UK (2021d) Government to Publish Levelling Up White Paper. [online] Available at: www.gov.uk/government/news/government-to-publish-levelling-up-white-paper (accessed 9 August 2022).

Gov.UK (2022) Discrimination: Your Rights. [online] Available at: www.gov.uk/discrimination-your-rights (accessed 8 August 2022).

Hayden, C and Jenkins, C (2014) 'Troubled Families' Programme in England: 'Wicked Problems' and Policy-Based Evidence. *Policy Studies*, 35(6): 631–49.

Horner, N (2019) *What is Social Work?* Exeter: Learning Matters.

Homelessness Act 2002 [online] Available at: www.legislation.gov.uk/ukpga/2002/7/contents (accessed 8 August 2022).

Homelessness Reduction Act 2017 [online] Available at: www.legislation.gov.uk/ukpga/2017/13/contents/enacted (accessed 8 August 2022).

Housing Act 1966 [online] Available at: www.legislation.gov.uk/ukpga/1996/52/contents (accessed 8 August 2022).

Khan, S, Combaz, E and Fraser, E (2015) Topic Guide on Social Exclusion (revised edition). Governance and Social Development Resource Centre (GSDRC), University of Birmingham. [online] Available at: www.gsdrc.org/go/topic-guides/social-exclusion (accessed 8 August 2022).

Kopczyk, K and Walker-Khan, M (2021) 10 people Share Their Experiences of Racism Across all Levels of the Game. *BBC News*. [online] Available at: www.bbc.co.uk/sport/extra/5v1pvdk8mr/Racism-in-football-our-stories (accessed 8 August 2022).

Lansley, M and Mack, J (2015) *Breadline Britain: The Rise of Mass Poverty*. London: Oneworld.

Levitas, R, Pantazis, C, Fahmy, E, Gordon, D, Lloyd, E and Patsios, D (2007) *The Multi-Dimensional Analysis of Social Exclusion*. Department of Sociology and School for Social Policy, Townsend Centre for the International Study of Poverty and Bristol Institute for Public Affairs, University of Bristol. [online] Available at: http://dera.ioe.ac.uk/6853/1/multidimensional.pdf (accessed 8 August 2022).

Llewellyn, A, Agu, L and Mercer, D (2014) *Sociology for Social Workers*. 2nd ed. Cambridge: Polity Press.

Marmot, M (Chair) (2010) Strategic Review of Health Inequalities in England post-2010. *Fair Society, Healthier Lives: The Marmot Review*. [online] Available at: https://eur02.safelinks.protection.outlook.com/?url=https%3A%2F%2Fwww.instituteofhealthequity.org%2Fresources-reports%2Fmarmot-review-10-years-on&data=05%7C01%7Cmhughes%40bournemouth.ac.uk%7C6e0f65a55d854df2c1a408da7a09def%7Cede29655d09742e4bbb5f38d427fbfb8%7C0%7C0%7C637956480031699787%7CUnknown%7CTWFpbGZsb3d8eyJWIjoiMC4wLjAwMDAiLCJQIjoiV2luMzIiLCJBTiI6Ik1haWwiLCJXVCI6Mn0%3D%7C3000%7C%7C%7C&sdata=RPl3RU8olX3G%2Fa2Hyy3SmWeoBPMa4LnOggZgj0nvyv0%3D&reserved=0 (accessed 8 August 2022).

Marmot, M (2020) Marmot Review 10 Years On. *British Medical Journal*, 368

Maslow, A H (1943) A Theory of Human Motivation. *Psychological Review*, 50(4), 370–96.

Moustafa, A A, Parkes, D, Fitzgerald, L, Underhill, D, Garami, J, Levy-Gigi, E, Stramecki, F, Valikhani, A, Frydecka, D and Misiak, B (2018) The Relationship between Childhood Trauma, Early-Life Stress, and Alcohol and Drug Use, Abuse, and Addiction: An Integrative Review. *Current Psychology*, 40, 579–84.

Murray, C (1996) *Charles Murray and the Underclass: The Developing Debate*. London: Civitas.

Office of National Statistics (ONS) (2021) Housing Affordability in England and Wales: 2020. [online] Available at: www.ons.gov.uk/peoplepopulationandcommunity/housing/bulletins/housingaffordabilityin englandandwales/2020 (accessed 8 August 2022).

No Fixed Address (anonymous author) (2017) 'The Big Stigma Is It's the Homeless Person's Fault'. *The Guardian*, 6 August 2017. [online] Available at: www.theguardian.com/society/2017/aug/07/the-big-sti gma-is-its-the-homeless-persons-fault (accessed 8 August 2022).

Pickett, K and Wilkinson, D (2010) *The Spirit Level*. London: Penguin.

Pierson, J (2016) *Tackling Poverty and Social Exclusion: Promoting Social Justice in Social Work*. 3rd ed. London: Routledge.

Pierson, J and Thomas, M (2013) *The Social Workers Guide to the Social Sciences. The Key Concepts.* Maidenhead. McGraw Hill.

Powell, A (2021) *NEET: Young People Not in Education, Employment or Training*. House of Commons Library. [online] Available at: https://researchbriefings.files.parliament.uk/documents/SN06705/SN06705.pdf (accessed 8 August 2022).

Putnam, R D (1995) Bowling Alone: America's Declining Social Capital. *Journal of Democracy*, 6(1): 65–78.

Shelter (2021) Legal Definition of Homelessness and Threatened Homelessness. [online] Available at: https://england.shelter.org.uk/professional_resources/legal/homelessness_applications/homelessness_ and_threatened_homelessness/legal_definition_of_homelessness_and_threatened_homelessness (accessed 9 August 2022).

Shildrick, T and Rucell, J (2015) *Sociological Perspective on Poverty*. Report for Joseph Rowntree Foundation. [online] Available at: www.jrf.org.uk/report/sociological-perspectives-poverty (accessed 8 August 2022).

Siegel, D, Smith, M C and Melucci, S C (2020) Teaching Social Work Students About Homelessness: An Interdisciplinary Interinstitutional Approach. *Journal of Social Work Education*, 56(S1): S59–71.

Social Exclusion Unit (2004) *Tackling Social Exclusion: Taking Stock and Looking to the Future. Emerging Findings*. London: Office of the Deputy Prime Minister.

Thompson, N (2021) *Anti-Discriminatory Practice*. 7th ed. London: Palgrave.

Trussell Trust (2021) End of Year Statistics. [online] Available at: www.trusselltrust.org/news-and-blog/lat est-stats/end-year-stats (accessed 8 August 2022).

United Nations (2016) *Leaving No One Behind: The Imperative of Inclusive Development*. New York: United Nations.

Warwick-Booth, L (2018) *Social Inequality*. 2nd ed. London: Sage.

Chapter 2 | Understanding stigma

Margarete Parrish

Chapter objectives

This chapter will help readers:

» understand the key theoretical perspectives relevant to understanding stigma;

» explore concepts of *internal vs. external attributions, locus of control* and *rationalisation*;

» understand factors leading to stigma and labelling;

» use reflective exercises to identify your own experiences of stigma and consider these in relation to others.

This chapter addresses some of the theoretical perspectives that relate to the consideration of stigma. The purpose of theory in this discussion is to provide a framework for understanding stigma in ways that serve to organise and structure ideas that contribute to a consistent and constructive approach. Theories provide a means of organising our ideas in order to explain and predict behaviours. In this case, we will be applying theories to explore how we understand the implications of stigma.

In order to discuss the relevant theories, some consideration of stigma is necessary. While various definitions may be used, for the purposes of this chapter, stigma is being considered around the concept of factors, experiences or features about which people feel somehow inferior to those around them. Goffman's classic work on stigma defined it as '*an attribute that is deeply discrediting*' (1963, p 3). Especially when considering the circumstances of people who are socially disadvantaged or excluded, we need to consider the possibility of our own perspectives being somehow biased. Those biases may be positive or negative, but they nonetheless demand consideration.

Stigma typically relates to a sense of shame that people feel when they regard themselves as not living up to other people's standards (Goffman, 1963). Importantly, shame typically reflects a sense of *being* flawed as opposed to *doing* something wrong, which makes for an important distinction. This important distinction is reflected in the sense of being very sorry about having stolen the cookies, which would indicate feeling *guilt*; feeling ashamed of *being a cookie thief*, however, is a more pervasive and profound sense of a flawed identity, which is relevant to the consideration of stigma.

Many factors or experiences can contribute to a person feeling somehow defective in comparison with others. Stigma may apply to individuals or groups. In a very appearance-focused society, such factors can range from being a few pounds overweight to not having the same expensive clothes that peers are wearing. For the purposes of this chapter and the rest of the book, stigma will be considered in relation to people who are socially excluded as a result of their lived experience and labels attributed to them.

Importantly, experiences that are associated with stigma are often difficult to discuss. They often involve factors that people do not readily disclose to others if it is not absolutely necessary to do so, sometimes out of fear of others' disapproval or scorn. Again, this often relates to a sense of shame or 'flawed-ness', rather than guilt. That is a large part of why it is so very important for helping professionals to appreciate the trust that is required for people to disclose and request help for such difficulties.

Goffman's classic work on stigma

No discussion of stigma or the theories that apply to it could be complete without consideration of Erving Goffman's classic work, *Stigma: Notes on the Management of Spoiled Identity* (1963). In that work, Goffman posits that stigma is by definition a social construct as opposed to an inherent attribute. According to Goffman, stigma represents a *'discrepancy between "virtual social identity" (how a person is characterised by society) and "actual social identity" (the attributes really possessed by a person'* (1963, p 2). Goffman's work focused particularly on the expectations that arise from stereotypes associated with stigma. Those stereotypes are typically defined around differences and the overt or covert devaluation of the person experiencing stigmatisation.

Attribution theory

One of the theoretical perspectives that is often relevant to the implications of bias is attribution theory. The key concepts of attribution theory are often found to be helpful in relation to how we find explanations for people's circumstances – either positive or negative. In everyday interactions with others, we often find ourselves in a position of making assessments or judgements (possibly assumptions) about the causes of behaviours and outcomes; our own as well as others'. Attribution theory relates to the ways in which we find explanations for people's circumstances. It may also serve as a way of rationalising that helps avoid the possibility that suffering harm or misfortune could be random or arbitrary, which would potentially put ourselves at risk of such misfortunes happening to us. By attributing blame or causation elsewhere, misfortune is made less random or uncontrollable, and thus less inescapable.

The ways in which we attribute causation and responsibility for various circumstances play essential roles in how we respond to the needs of people experiencing those circumstances. If our attributions tend to be negative, our responses are more likely to be suspicious or guarded, or even blaming. If our attributions are more contextual and essentially positive, then our responses are likely to be more compassionate and constructive. Hence an awareness of our own attributional patterns and styles can prove essential to good practice.

Reflective activity

Take a moment to apply this to your own life.

» Are there groups within society that you have judged negatively or blamed for their situation? Are there groups in society that you tend to look upon more favourably?

» How does this affect your compassion for them?

» Does your attitude towards this group vary according to other factors, such as gender, age or ethnicity?

» Do you really know anything about their situation or circumstances?

Attribution theory has evolved from the work of multiple theorists, particularly from Harold Kelley (1971, 1992) and Bernard Weiner (1986). The theory's primary focus is on how individuals gather and structure their beliefs about the causation of various behaviours or events. According to attribution theory, most people are consistently inclined to attribute their own circumstances or behaviours to *internal* factors, while they are typically inclined to attribute others' circumstances or behaviours to *external* factors (Passer and Smith, 2011).

By attributing causation to something other than 'fate' or any other arbitrary factor, individuals are also finding ways of organising their beliefs in ways that tend to diminish the anxieties that are likely to accompany the sense that suffering is random and unavoidable. Weiner (1986) proposed that causation could be placed along several dimensions, including internal and external. Internal or personal attributions infer that those events or circumstances are determined by personal/internal characteristics. An example would be: *'No one in my family caught Covid because we observed all the precautions and had our immunisations.'* Such beliefs are also linked with having an internal *locus of control.* A more external or situational attributional style would entail identifying events or circumstances that were externally influenced by factors typically outside the individual's control. An example would be: *'They caught Covid because they live in a bad neighbourhood and went to parties and concerts.'* Again, such beliefs typically reflect an external locus of control. Some examples are provided in Table 2.1.

Table 2.1 Examples of internal and external causation

Internal causation	External causation
Genetic or inherited characteristics (positive or negative)	Environmental influences and factors: air pollution, bad diet, socio-economic factors, etc
Inherent traits or characteristics	Negative peer influence; bad environment
Personal diligence; hard work	Supernatural powers (luck, fate, angels…)
Preparation, planning	Chance
Personal organisation/disorganisation	Situational factors – structural support vs chaos; privilege vs disadvantages

Internal and external causations are sometimes also referred to as personal and situational attributions. Personal (internal) attributions typically reflect a belief that behaviours or circumstances have been determined by individuals' characteristics. An (internal) example would be *'They drink too much because they lack the willpower to know when to stop'*, as opposed to *'they drink too much in order to fit in with their social group'* (external attribution). Situational (external) attributions typically reflect a belief that an individual's external circumstances have influenced or determined their behaviours or circumstances.

Attributions of causation are also linked with the concept of locus of control. When referring to locus of control, the focus is typically linked with the individual's perception of where or what the strongest influence is when considering behaviour or outcome. For example, when employing an internal locus of control, a student might decide not to go out clubbing with their flatmates tonight because they are giving a class presentation tomorrow, and they want to be at their best. When employing an external locus of control, that student might decide that their flatmates would be really disappointed, and possibly disapproving, if they didn't go clubbing with the group. An internal locus of control is generally associated with a sense of autonomy, or such concepts as Bandura's (1977, 1986) idea of self-efficacy.

Attributions play an important role in shaping our expectations and explanations of people's circumstances and outcomes. An example could be a student's response to grades received on a test. If their grade is higher than they expected, do they attribute that to having studied hard (internal or personal causations) or to luck or the test being easier than expected (external or situational causations)? If others made higher grades than themselves, do they attribute that to others having worked hard or to luck?

By definition, attribution theory involves some consideration of context. The application of attribution theory necessarily reflects to some degree how a person considers the role of context in relation to behaviours and outcomes. Are those behaviours and outcomes reflective of personal strengths or weaknesses, or are they reflective of environmental factors? Because of its inherent relevance to working with people experiencing disadvantages (including those associated with stigma), the importance of understanding and considering the role of context in people's circumstances is intrinsically linked with the applicability of attribution theory when working with people experiencing hardships. Attributions may influence both their own perceptions of their circumstances as well as others' responses to them – either positively or negatively.

In keeping with the basic function of theories, attribution theory plays a key role in shaping expectations and explanations of people's circumstances and experiences. It often contributes to predictions of outcomes when anticipating results of people's behaviours. Such factors are crucial in how professionals maintain an awareness of their own attributional style and possible bias.

Negative internal attributions are often associated with circumstances involving stigma. When applying negative internal attributions to explain someone's circumstances, the reasoning typically relies on considering some inherent weakness or flaw on that person's part that explains their difficulties. Some people would consider this a form of 'blaming the victim'.

Table 2.2 provides some routine social examples for you to consider, along with your own further thoughts about stereotypes and expectations.

Table 2.2 Examples of negative internal and external attributions

Circumstances	Negative internal attribution	Negative external attribution	Further thoughts?
Using a food bank	They are choosing to use the food bank so that they can spend their money on expensive phones.	The costs of living are now forcing people to ask for help that they previously could afford for themselves.	
Being homeless	Their drinking/drug use has made them unsuitable tenants.	Losing their job during the pandemic has meant that they also lost their housing.	
Young person undergoing sexual transition	They are just doing this because they've seen it on the news.	Pursuing such an option must require tremendous courage in order to cope with the social pressures involved.	
Domestic abuse between partners	She should have known better than to get involved with such a character as that.	Growing up in violent families has contributed to some very frightening norms for both partners.	
Cases of university students being drunk in public	*'Boys will be boys.'* *'What a disgrace for girls to be so drunk.'*	Inexperienced young drinkers are often targeted by the alcohol industry with cheap drinks that are also high in alcohol content.	
Cases of 'date rape'	She must have done something that brought this on.	He must have spiked her drink.	

Another example could be found when working with someone who is drug dependent; understanding their attributions of causation will typically prove essential to understanding their expectations of the outcome of usage. If someone has positive expectations of their drug use ('desired consequences'), then they are more likely to employ positive attributions to their usage. Examples could include such views as '*It relaxes me*', or '*It isn't a problem*'. Examples of negative attributions ('undesired outcomes') could include such expectations as '*It would mean that I can't control my usage'*, or *'It would place me in danger from harm'*. When working alongside people experiencing such difficulties, understanding the differences in people's attributions and expectations is essential.

Role theory

Similarly, role theory may play an important part in how people perceive and anticipate behaviour and circumstances. Social roles may be positive or negative. They are sometimes ascribed according to relationships (parents, partners, siblings, etc). They may also reflect associations with function (students, lecturers, police, politicians). They may be positive or negative, and they may reflect stereotypes and possible bias. While some roles are associated with positive bias, or positive attributions, others can be more problematic.

When roles are associated with stigma, the linkages between roles and attributions may become complex. For example, on a positive level, a student who has done very well on an in-class test may attain the role of a desirable study partner when preparing for the final essay. A student who has disclosed a history of drug use when they were younger may find that they are assigned a role of being unreliable or an undesirable colleague, regardless of justification. Such biases and stereotypes interface with attributions – positive or negative – in relation to expectations of self or others.

Role theory is often linked with labelling. Again, stereotypes may play a powerful part in attributing roles. For example, when working with someone who has a history of mental health crises, a role may have evolved for them to behave erratically, or to be dependent on others for their care. Such stereotypes or labels (such as *crazy* or *schizo*) may combine with social stigma in ways that deter people from their fulfilling their actual potential. One way of trying to minimise the risk of labelling people in conversations or in writing is to be careful to always to refer to their humanity before their condition. For example, referring to 'people with mental health problems' rather than 'psychiatric cases' places the person before the condition. Likewise, 'people with drug dependence' would be preferable to 'drug addicts'.

Prejudice in relation to stigma is a powerful component of a variety of types of social injustice. An awareness of how complex people's circumstances can be can prove to be an important starting point for avoiding bias, stereotypes and unfounded attributions. An awareness of how stigma can shape both people's experiences as well as their sense of self is an essential tool when working with or encountering people facing social exclusion.

These theories provide a useful lens through which to view and reflect on the following chapters and lived experiences.

References

Bandura, A (1977) Self-Efficacy: Toward a Unifying Theory of Behavior Change. *Psychological Review*, 84(2): 191–215.

Bandura, A (1986) *Social Foundations of Thought and Action.* Englewood Cliffs, NJ: Prentice Hall.

Goffman, I (1963) *Stigma: Notes on the Management of Spoiled Identity.* Englewood Cliffs, NJ: Prentice Hall.

Kelley, H (1971) Attribution in Social Interaction. In Jones, E E, Kanouse, D E, Kelley, H H, Nisbett, R E, Valins, S and Weiner, B (eds) *Attribution: Perceiving the Causes of Behaviour* (pp 1–26). Morristown, NJ: Lawrence Erlbaum Associates.

Kelley, H (1992) Common-Sense Psychology and Scientific Psychology. In Rosenzweig, M and Porter, L (eds) *Annual Review of Psychology*, vol 43 (pp 1–23). Sao Paulo, CA: Annual Reviews.

Passer, M and Smith, R (2011) *Psychology: Science of Mind and Behaviour.* 5th ed. Maidenhead: McGraw-Hill.

Weiner, B (1986) *An Attibutional Theory of Motivation and Emotion.* New York: Springer.

Chapter 3 | Being in care

Shannon Cullen and Richard Williams

My name is Shannon and I am a 25-year-old care leaver who got placed into care around the age of 18 months. I was young enough to be adopted and my brother to be fostered; however, my paternal grandmother and step-grandad could not watch me and my brother being split up so stood in 'temporarily' to be our legal guardians. As I said, temporarily; this meant that our parents were given the opportunity to receive help and support in order to meet the needs that us as children required.

Grandparents

In 2017, there were 258,600 households with a grandparent as the head of the household in the UK, which was 3.2 per cent of households with dependent children (ONS, 2022) – this is the equivalent of one child in every classroom.

Being young, I do not remember much; however, I have done life story work and have heard a lot about my past. We were a serious case of neglect: we were constantly dirty; we had no food. Milk vouchers and food vouchers were sold so that my parents could buy their next 'fix' and I had to attend hospital for a bad case of boils on my bottom, which was the result of being left in dirty nappies for long periods of time.

Everybody has always said that I was so miserable as all I done as a child was cry, no matter what. Even if I was doing something nice. My nan believes to this day that I was born addicted to heroin; I showed all of the signs of withdrawal for many years. I mean, add this to being taken away from your parents and being hungry; of course I was going to be miserable. Wouldn't anybody?

I was such an angry child; I hated everybody and everything. Growing up I couldn't understand, why me? What had I done wrong to deserve so much pain throughout my life? Why did my parents not love me enough to care for me? All throughout my life it has been empty promises, promises of going back to live with my parents. Promises that my parents would become clean. Promises that they loved me. Promises that they would stop breaking the law. All these promises just became pointless words after a while, as I soon discovered they were not going to change. One part of my court file says 'Shannon is too young to express her wishes and feelings'; they just didn't listen.

Attachment and the school's role

If a child's experience is that their needs are unmet, the child may be unable to build a secure and stable bond with their parents or guardians. This may then lead to the child developing an insecure attachment style and ultimately an unhealthy understanding of how relationships work. It has also been linked to behavioural problems such as attention deficit hyperactivity disorder (ADHD) or conduct disorder (Fearon et al, 2010).

School can be – and should be – a place of safety; somewhere to make and be with friends. For a child living through trauma outside school, this can be a real challenge that compounds their sense of isolation. Bergin and Bergin (2009) found, for children with insecure attachment, that sustaining good relationships requires particular teachers and other school staff to have skills to address children's distrust of adults and their challenging behaviour.

How can we help? The following quote may invite pause for thought:

Do these pupils really need more access to study opportunities, better teaching, different reading schemes, more computers, more effective discipline? What if they just needed more access to you and to me? A genuine relationship. Is this a possibility? What if it really wasn't more complicated than that? What if the tool that we had overlooked – ourselves – was the bridge into a world of possibilities, that a genuine relationship with us, perhaps acting as a buffer, could switch on the pupil's 'thinking brain' and integrate it with his 'emotional brain'?

(Bomber and Hughes, 2013)

Throughout the younger years of my life, I constantly waited around the phone. Longing for that phone call from my parents to hear their voice and to tell them I loved them and to hear it back, regardless of how much pain they had caused... all I wanted was them. It's normal. And I know that now. Every child wants their parents, no matter what turmoil they have put you through. It is a natural instinct to feel love for the people that put you on the earth. Due to the complete ignorance and inconsistency of my parents, phone calls at one point were at a scheduled time of the day so I would know when to expect a call. This was to enable me to live my life, but I still did not want to. I would sit and wait for the phone to ring, but some days it never did. I would miss out on playing with friends or doing after-school activities because talking to my mum, to me, was more important. Having no phone calls often left me living in constant fear – were they dead, were they hurt? Regardless of whether they were or not, I have basically had to already grieve for parents who are still alive.

Education was always the main focus throughout my life, if not from myself then from everybody else. I can remember being on report in first school, Year 4, for my behaviour; I needed my teachers to understand me as a child in care. I was not naughty and I was not a trouble-maker. I needed extra support within certain areas of my life and as a child I did not know this. It should have been professionals picking up on the need for extra support and teaching me vital skills that would benefit my behaviour such as learning how to build correct attachments, understanding negative situations and learning how to control feelings. This would have all helped throughout many stages of my life. This followed through to middle school; however, I picked up a love for PE, which seemed to control any negative behaviour... until I was able to understand life and become my own person.

Upper school, this was the worst stage of my life. I was changing; I was realising things I had never realised before. I was becoming independent. I wanted my mum more than ever. My behaviour was awful throughout this stage of my life; I was so close to being kicked out of school in Year 9. I was often in isolation and I just did not care. I was not fussed about completing school; I just wanted to mess around.

There was a SENCO (Special Educational Needs Co-ordinator) room known as A3 at the school that I went to. I got on really well with the teacher; he knew my brother and understood our lives. It was a room that you would go to when you found a lesson too overwhelming. I took every advantage of this I could. I think that they should have been stricter with me instead of just pussyfooting around me, scared to say something and upset me. I would just mess around and play on my phone; I never really got any work done.

In Year 10 I was put into a 'special' group to help with my GCSEs; it was to help gain five A–Cs and was for people who had experienced difficulties. Some of my major lessons were dropped such as biology, physics and chemistry and replaced with 'simpler' subjects such as sports science, food science and forensic science. Although it was a well-supported group, it was just another thing that made me stand out.

Attainment

When we compare the attainment of looked after children with the general population of children, the wealth of government data (DfE, 2020) includes the following.

» In 2019, at the end of Key Stage 2, 37 per cent of looked after children reached the expected standard in the headline measure reading, writing and maths, which is much lower than the 65 per cent for non-looked after children.

» Progress 8 aims to capture the progress a pupil makes from the end of Key Stage 2 to the end of Key Stage 4; it compares pupils' achievement – their Attainment 8 score – with the national average. In 2019, the average Attainment 8 score for looked after children was 19.1 compared to 44.6 for non-looked after children and 19.2 for children in need.

» Crucially, there is also clear evidence that looked after children have a significantly higher rate of special educational needs (SEN) than the general population. Looked after children and children in need reaching the end of Key Stage 4 are three to four times more likely to have an SEN than all children and this is likely to have a major impact on their attainment.

» For university entrance, in 2018–19 only 13 per cent of pupils who were looked after continuously for 12 months or more entered higher education compared to 43 per cent of all other pupils.

Growing up was tough; I never understood why people did not want to play with me and why parents did not want me to play with their children. I was the same as everyone else; it was my parents that were different and troubled, but I often got the backlash from it. To be able to go over to a friend's house, anyone over 18 would have to have a CRB (Criminal Records Bureau check) now called Disclosure and Barring Service check (DBS) before I could go. This meant that I had to plan majorly in advance, meaning I often missed out on the late notice *'Do you want to come to my house tonight?'* – I'd have to say no and explain why, while explaining everything if they didn't already know my situation. It was tough because I was never allowed on holiday with my friends; I often missed out if my social worker did not apply for the CRB quick enough. I often needed extra permission to be able to do fun activities such as school trips or bowling as risk assessments needed to be done.

Looked after children (LAC) reviews have always been a pain in the ass to be honest. I have always felt like another number, a statistic. Imagine sitting in a room full of professionals that are all talking about you and not to you. I was often bribed to attend these with sweets because they were so boring, and not what you want to be doing when you have been at school for seven hours. My days were often overtaken with writing and reading letters either from my parents or another professional. I had my own LAC nurse, which was good, yes, as I had a positive relationship with her, and she was consistent but none of my friends had their 'own' nurse and they didn't have to have health checks every six weeks.

I had to tell my social worker everything: who I played with and what I had done. They used to come over every six weeks after school, which prevented me from being social and playing with my friends. I remember requesting a computer, which was agreed as it was for my learning; however, I had to go on an internet safety course to be allowed it, which was so embarrassing to tell my friends. I had to do it on a Saturday, which again stopped me from being social.

Support

How effectively any school supports a child who is experiencing trauma can be life changing. The lack of meaningful support can all too easily lead to exclusion. By way of contrast, Romano et al (2015) argue that children need a positive culture of expectations, an environment that deals sensitively with trauma and this within a structured routine that the child can experience as fair.

While looked after children are over five times more likely to have a fixed-period exclusion than the general population of children (GPC), the rate of permanent exclusions for looked after children has decreased and is now lower than the rate for GPC.

Looked after children are almost four times more likely to have a special educational need (SEN) than GPC and are almost nine times more likely to have an education, health and care plan than GPC. Crucially, looked after children with either with no identified SEN or who receive SEN support typically progress as well or better than non-looked after children (DfE, 2020). This indicates that targeting appropriate SEN support to looked after children is essential to promote their attainment.

During my early teenage years, I started to visit my mum unsupervised, as I longed for a relationship so badly with her. Little did I know that she was just going to manipulate me: take money from me for drugs, promising she would give it back. I was sneaking off to visit her until my nan found out, which pushed her over the edge and she asked for myself and my brother to be removed. This happened very quickly. I can remember the social worker coming to get us and taking us to a temporary foster placement. One hour and a half away from everything. Everything I had ever known; everyone I had ever known and everyone I loved. It was just me and my brother, alone, somewhere we had never been before, and we were scared. We did not know these people, and we were not given the chance to meet them before we were taken there. Our social worker drove us there, introduced us and off he went. This was the worst social worker I have experienced and, believe me, I have had a lot, 30 plus, as far as I can remember. I even went a period of time without a social worker at all.

Inconsistency

Inconsistency in their care is associated with negative developmental outcomes for young people in care (Sattler et al, 2018). This can lead to poorer outcomes and isolation. We can see from the national data that (in)consistency of care is a significant issue. A report from the Children's Commissioner for England (2019) from 2016–17 to 2017–18 found more than half (55 per cent) of children saw their social worker change twice or more, while for 32 per cent it was three or more times. A 'large amount of variation' in the levels of social worker instability could not be explained by workforce, child or placement factors, but was associated with poorer Ofsted ratings.

He made me feel so uncomfortable because it was clear that he did not care. On the way to the foster placement, he barely spoke to us; when he dropped us off, he barely spoke to us. He didn't tell us anything: how long we would be here; if we were going to move back closer to home; if my school was going to change. He left me feeling more confused than ever. I felt so alone in this place, and he did not help to settle me in any way. I would have appreciated a text from him to see how we were doing, but he just done nothing. Even if he was to text me, I wouldn't have been able to get it anyway.

A complaint went in, and I asked for a new social worker.

Just take a second, as the reader, to imagine feeling alone, somewhere you have never been before in your life, with people you have never met in your life. Now, all of a sudden you are supposed to call this place 'home'; these strangers are now your carers and have a say in pretty much everything that you do, and you have to stay in a room that has no personal connection to yourself with none of your personal items in it apart from either the black bag or suitcase that you had to pack. Scary, isn't it?

Experiences of moving home

Downie and Twomey (2022) found that in 2020 there were 184 complaints made by children in care against councils related to moving home. Making a complaint when feeling vulnerable, not knowing what will happen, feeling overwhelmed – that can be a very isolated place. The National Youth Advocacy Service (NYAS) also found that four in five looked after children have their possessions moved in bin bags when they change homes. Both multiple placements and frequent changes in foster care increase the predicted probability of high use of mental health services (Rubin et al, 2004).

It was during this time that my mum decided to use somebody's phone from the night shelter in our hometown to contact me on various occasions. Little did I know that this person turned out to be a paedophile. I can remember the police coming in to school to talk to me about it and to confiscate my phone for investigation. I didn't understand any of it because I did not receive anything indecent; however, I understand now that it was to be cautious towards my safety. Even throughout this, there was no extra support from my social worker. This man had broken every piece of trust that I had for men, which wasn't much anyway. But he just reinforced my thoughts that I couldn't trust men.

Relationships with teachers and social workers

From this isolated place, it adds clarity to Shannon's sense of isolation to remember that children look for care and reciprocity in their relationships with social workers and teachers and this can be achieved through listening and small acts of kindness. Children are adept at recognising aspects of social workers' and others' verbal and non-verbal communications which indicate to the child whether they are listening and interested in them. Gorin et al (2021) found that children are particularly vulnerable if parents are resistant to engagement or if children's trust is broken.

During this time, I was still attending school. Unfortunately for my brother, who is three years older than me and was around 15 at this time, he had to spend all day every day, alone and scared in this strange new home with the foster carer. An hour-and-a-half taxi journey for me every morning and every afternoon; three hours of my day wasted travelling to and from school. I couldn't deal with it, I didn't want to deal with it, so I didn't. I remember coming home one day and packing a bag, saying that I was going to the shop and turning my phone off. I was gone; I was free. I ran away for two days, hurt a lot of people and broke a lot of hearts, but I needed to get my point across. I was not happy. I was 12 years old. Once I agreed to come back and meet the police, they put me in a cell while I had to wait for an out-of-hours social worker to arrive to decide what they were going to do with me. I felt invisible while they were talking about me; they were not listening, and this social worker seemed as though he did not care. He just wanted to go home at the end of the day. Well, good for him, he had a home. He had somewhere that he could feel safe and secure. But where was my home? I felt so small, and I just wanted to die.

Social exclusion

In their study published in 2012, Jackson and Cameron (2012) found that social workers' low expectations and lack of interest in education was a key factor in the attainment of looked after children and consequently their experience of social exclusion as adults. In addition, looked after children – precisely as Shannon has described in her own experience – may have many social workers, so perhaps it is inevitable that relationships may some-times break down. This can worsen their sense of 'being alone' without meaningful support. Nevertheless, as Gorin et al (2021) found, the social worker is an important figure, and children need opportunities to develop new relationships with social workers when previous relationships have broken down

I can remember spending the majority of my time in my bedroom; I withdrew myself from society and everyone that loved me. I would sit in my room and listen to music, I think trying to escape the reality of life at times. The year 2009 I hit rock bottom mentally and at 13 years of age I tried to end my life; I couldn't cope, I didn't want to cope and I didn't understand what I had done wrong through life to deserve so much heartache. This is when CAMHS (Child and Adolescent Mental Health Services) began to be involved. I had my first appointment, and I was so nervous. I walked in, sat down and the man just stared at me waiting for me to talk. This is not what I wanted, so I got up, walked out and refused to see him again. Luckily, I was listened to, and I was given a new therapist named Claire who was absolutely incredible. She really understood me and wanted the best for me. She had worked with my brother for a little bit so already understood a lot of things, which was an advantage. She helped me to unpick a lot of things and taught me different ways to control my emotions. She went above and beyond for me; I'm not sure what it was but we had such a connection. I'm not sure if it was because she put so much time into me or because we just clicked, but I know she helped a hell of a lot.

While at school, the SENCO worker (a school teacher who is responsible for planning and monitoring the progress of children with special educational needs and disabilities), the youth worker and my deputy head of year invited a group in to help with children who were feeling low. The group was called the KORU project, run by a lady called Andrea Moran. Now this lady, I can honestly say... saved my life. She was what I needed. The group was a drama and arts-based therapy group, and it was amazing. I did not want it to end, so when it did, Andrea applied for individual funding which was awarded, and we started working together on a one-to-one basis. Andrea taught me so much, she opened my eyes to real life, she was honest with me. She gave me an insight into her own life, meaning that we could connect on a personal basis. She allowed me to be who I was; if I wanted to swear, I could; if I wanted to cry, scream, shout, I could; sometimes she even joined in with me. It was little things as well; she made me feel wanted, loved; she gave me something to look forward to, every week. I will never forget the burn box. We wrote down every name of everyone who has ever upset or hurt me and put them in a fire pit and set fire to every single name. The relief from this was insane. I felt so powerful and uplifted. This is when my life began to change.

Championing looked after children

Jackson and Cameron (2012) found that often, a champion – either in school, in foster care or in the local authority – had made a critical difference to self-belief.

Glyde's (2014) reflection upon her experience as a therapist is that she has lost count of the number of times a child has expressed in therapy that '*I just want to be normal*' and she discusses how isolating it can be to be 'different'.

Notice that I haven't spoken about my dad much? Well, that's because most of my childhood I have spent visiting him in prisons. I have travelled half the country to visit him; I have missed out on education to visit him. I longed for these visits though; I would be so excited to see him and to spend time with him. If I wasn't seeing my dad in prison, I would be visiting him in rehab, hospital or mental health facilities. This was scary. Not just scary seeing my dad in these places but also scary seeing everybody else. Everybody is different and has a different story to tell and knowing that I was in a visiting room full of criminals from such a young age is terrifying. I travelled half the country to visit my mum in prisons, rehabs and hospitals too. My social worker took us most of the time. Missing out on weekends/evenings due to travelling to prisons, rehabs and mental health hospitals.

When a parent is in prison

In a study by Raikes published in 2016, it was found that pressures faced by grandparent carers of children with incarcerated parents occur as a result of stigma, loss, isolation, poor health and a lack of practical, emotional and financial support. According to the National Information Centre on Children of Offenders (Kincaid et al, 2019), an estimated 310,000 children every year have a parent in prison in England and Wales and 10,000 visits are made by children to public prisons every week.

This has made me question so much about why I was taken to such scary places from such a young age. I do not recall being asked if I wanted to go and even if I had been asked, would a two or three or even four year-old really understand the question being asked? These places were no place for a child to be and for my social worker to not only be agreeing to these visits but taking me is beyond me. Like I have said, I have always longed for my parents and wanted them so badly and I completely understand that the child's needs are paramount – a key principle of the Children Act 1989 – but were my needs being met here, or were my parents' needs being met? I mean, yes, I wanted to see my parents; however, it never done me any good seeing them as I was always destructive after visits. Looking back now, I see this as institutional abuse from social services; they were putting my parents' needs before my own.

This is when my mental health got worse. I was going through my GCSEs at school while still trying to help my mum, be there for her. I was basically parenting her. I remember constantly being on the phone to my mum while her partner at the time was beating her. They were homeless and were staying in a hotel. I can remember hearing him trying to kick the door down that she was hiding behind in the bathroom. She was hysterical; I couldn't get any sense out of her apart from her asking me to contact the police, so I did. However, I didn't know where she was, what hotel she was in. I was on my mobile phone to my mum in my left ear and 999 on the house phone to my right ear in early hours of the morning. This happened on numerous occasions. I witnessed it visually many times on visits.

Social services have always taken myself and my brother on visits when they know what the outcomes will be. My mum was in an abusive relationship for many years; they knew this. I remember making my mum a birthday cake and taking it to her. We met her at a bowling alley. It was usually at birthdays or Christmas that we would do something special. Before I knew it, her partner was running around the corner, drunk, ready to argue and beat her up. Instead, he decided he would punch the cake and throw it on the floor, rip up the cards for my mum and lose it. Within minutes we were removed and taken home. Everybody was looking at us; it was so embarrassing. Even more so when my mum would turn up with bags of presents and we would have to open them on the train station platform or in a café. I mean, it was lovely to receive these, but we weren't allowed to always keep them because more often than not, they were stolen. When I attended unsupervised, I can remember watching my mum's partner physically beat my mum, smashing a radio over her head and attempting to smash through her kitchen window. I couldn't deal with it and got physical with him. He contacted the police and luckily they knew my mum and her partner very well and understood that I was protecting my mum.

It's just crazy though, how social services knew how most of our visits went and when things got too bad they would take us away from contact. It was as if they were tormenting us every time, as if giving a lollipop to a child and taking it away. They were making us relive our childhood all over again, making us leave our parents under negative circumstances. Why did they still provide the contact when they were fully aware of what it would do to us? We often saw violence, drugs and my parents were often drunk or high on something, but the visits still continued as I got older.

One thing I hate to talk about, something that destroyed me for many years, but is a huge part of my story and the reason I am who I am today. I was sexually abused by someone who lived very close to our family home, a family friend. It started when I was around eight and finished when I reported it, which was when I was 12 or 13. I can remember going to social services with two other girls who had reported it too. We were sat in a room and questioned. We had the day off school. The next thing we had to do was to go to the police station for a camera statement. The police were very aware of this person, knew what he was like and were desperate to get him. While the investigation was ongoing, I had to stay away from my home, mainly for my own safety.

I had to stay at my maternal grandmother's for a while, which was horrible. I felt so out of place and alone. Anyway, the day came when we were being given the verdict: was the CPS (Crown Prosecution Service) going to accept it or not? This day broke my heart as they had decided to not take it further as one of the girls had lied and, within days of telling the police, she was going back around to the family's home. I think this is when I went through the worst stage of my life as all I wanted to do was hurt this other person. She was actually meant to be one of my best friends. She disappeared for a long time; I had therapy and I realised I'm better than this and stronger than this.

Well-being support

Hannah Marsden (2017) led a study commissioned by Barnardo's into the *'wellbeing of children involved in criminal justice processes relating to sexual exploitation and abuse'*. One very clear finding was that the benefits of consistent, one-to-one support from an independent, voluntary sector specialist worker were crucial to the promotion of children and young people's well-being, and to supporting them onto a pathway to recovery

This was such a difficult time as so many people were angry. A lot of people understood what this person was like, and many didn't. I think a lot of people thought I wasn't telling the truth, but I'm the most truthful person you could come across, I mean that's easy for me to say, but I wouldn't be writing this chapter now if I wasn't truthful. It's frustrating, because even now I'm still trying to prove myself, and for who, for what? I know what happened; I remember the details vividly and for anyone who wants to argue it, I can sit them down and tell them every inch of what happened. Wow, that was hard to talk about. I'm not sure if you can feel my anger there; I just feel so betrayed and small, even now years later. I can remember the shame, going back into school the next day. Everybody by this time had heard and people were looking and talking about me. Not everything was bad. Some people were trying to pity me and feel sorry for me, which is something I do not like. I have never seen myself as a victim and I never will.

It was hard because everybody knew what my parents had done. Where I am from is a small town, and everybody knows each other so most people knew my situation. Many people were aware of what happened to us as children and our surname is known to many people and professionals, which often left me feeling judged when they would talk about what had happened or asked questions about my parents.

My parents (more so my mum) have begged most of their lives, and have actually asked some of my friends for money on occasions. It is so embarrassing seeing them on the street begging, especially when they use me as a motive. Many times, my mum has said that she needed to visit her children with the money and then my friends would ask me how the visit went, the visit I had no idea about. It always left me feeling so unloved, to be used, even when we weren't in contact. It is also a normal occurrence for people to tell me that they saw my parents the other day, and how bad they looked. It makes me feel so ashamed that people know who they are and gives me so many thoughts about what they are doing.

I have often seen my parents in the newspaper, more so with technology growing. Seeing the comments that people put on the articles was awful, saying how they should be murdered and tortured and how they are vermin. It breaks my heart. Although they have done me harm, they are still my parents, and it is soul destroying reading comments like this. At the end of the day, they are still human; they still have needs, feelings and people who care. It is honestly so confusing having feelings like this because part of me hates them for what they have done to us, but I do not wish harm upon anyone and they gave me life, experiences etc.

I often think about how different life would have been if I had been adopted: I would not have been abused by this person; I wouldn't have visited so many institutions; I wouldn't have witnessed so many scenes of domestic abuse; I wouldn't have had drugs smoked in front of me; I wouldn't have been bullied for being 'the druggies' child'; I wouldn't have had as much support throughout school; I probably would have come across as 'normal'; I may not have had so much anger growing up and I would have been wanted and loved. But then also, if my parents didn't put drugs before me, I would have had a normal childhood.

Children Act 1989

A key principle of the Children Act 1989 is that children are best looked after within their families, with their parents playing a full part in their lives. A court removing a child from their parents must only be done when absolutely necessary. In terms of the provision a looked after child may then be offered, the report *An International Perspective of Fostering and Adoption Outcomes* by Pritchard et al (2018) concluded that residential care often achieves more than realised, fostering is better than residential care, kinship care is likely to improve outcomes further and that adoption broadly shades the other options, if permanent out-of-home care is necessary.

I saw so much throughout my childhood. I missed out on so much too. I had to grow up before my age; I had to mature a lot earlier than a lot of people I know as they had been wrapped in cotton wool and hidden from the real world. I missed out on vital education from visiting my parents in hospitals, prisons and rehabs. I missed out on making friends and growing up like a child. I was often teased for having 'druggie' parents. I got bullied a few times for this, more so in first school as children did not understand. I got bullied once in middle school for it. I soon dealt with it my own way but got in trouble for it. I often felt embarrassed to tell people things about my life.

People would make their minds up about me before they even got a chance to know me. It was often very difficult to break down their barriers due to the public perception and stigma associated with children in care.

Right to privacy

Children have a right to privacy, and this includes how they share information. In a study of 80 children aged 8–18 years in informal kinship care (being placed with family), Farmer et al (2013) found that of those who did not share information about their backgrounds with other children, almost two-thirds had parents with drug misuse problems and one in five had a parent who was in prison.

Growing up, I blamed my nan for everything. My mum had drummed it into my head that she 'stole' us from her, which I believed. My behaviour was disgusting; there was no excuse for it at times. However, I was trying to find my place on the earth. Once I decided to move out into supported lodgings at age 17, my relationship with nan blossomed. I realised how much she had done for me and how much support I had from her. We have a lovely relationship now; she is my best friend. I am so thankful for everything she and my step-grandad have done for both me and my brother as we could be anywhere if it wasn't for them. They gave up their whole lives for us and I could never, ever repay them for the love and affection that they showed us throughout our lives.

Moving out at 17 into supported lodging, I never felt at home. My room was old school and not very modern. I had no choice but to claim benefits, which made me feel so small. When I left, things were not great and when I went to collect my items, everything was packed ready for me.

I met my son's father in 2012 and I remember him meeting my mum for the first time and just saying to me, '*Why are you wasting your life on this!?*' At this stage my life changed for the better. I fell pregnant and gave birth in 2017 to my beautiful, cheeky son, Carlos. He completed me. He taught me how to love again. He taught me so much. He also broke me at times. He made me realise how innocent children are, how they do not deserve half of the stuff that they go through. He made me think about my own childhood and wonder how my parents could do what they done to me. He made me contemplate life. He made me strong and he made me into the person I am today. The hardest part was when he was 18 months old. It reminded me of how young I was when I was placed into care. How small I was, how I didn't do anything wrong. He made me want to do better. So, I did. I went back to college in 2019 to complete the Access to Health Professions Diploma to enable myself to go on to university and become a social worker. To be able to enable people to feel loved and love themselves.

I feel quite lucky to be honest, as I have been able to mentally block out a lot of memories from my past. I feel for my brother as he saw so much and has been so badly failed by the system. He saw so much more than me and has been pushed from pillar to post by services, leaving him screaming for help. It is heartbreaking that I can receive so much help and support, but he didn't and still isn't. My heart breaks for him. I will always wonder what my life would or could have been like if social services chose a different path for me, or if my nan and step-grandad didn't take us in. I owe my nan and step-grandad so much. Unfortunately, my step-grandad passed away the day before my interview for university; however, I believe he was with me as he got me through it. All I can do is try and make my nan and step-grandad proud of me. I honestly owe them the world. If it wasn't for them both, I could be anywhere around the country, or even dead. Who knows? They stepped up to be my parents; they nurtured me, fed me, loved me and showed me what a family unit was. I can only regret my behaviour in the past and the way I treated my nan at times. I was evil throughout my teenage years; I am just so grateful that they never gave up on us. I can honestly say that my nan is my hero and I love her to pieces.

Leaving care – aged 25 – who do I turn to? Where do I turn? I have had help and support all of my life, and then when I turn a certain age leaving care services stop working with me. It makes me feel similar to how I felt growing up. I feel as though I am being abandoned all over again. Who says that because you turn 25, your parents come back into your life? Just because you turn a certain age it does not mean that you no longer need support. Structured support has been a priority all of my life. I have always felt below all of my family, as though my parents' mistakes are my problem. I have felt like the black sheep many times.

Leaving **care**

Provision for children leaving care and transitioning into independence is backed up by legislation, including the Children (Leaving Care) Act 2000; by government guidance to local authorities including 'Extending Personal Adviser Support to all Care Leavers to Age 25' (DfE, 2018). But all of these are put into context by Ofsted's (2022) research '"Ready or Not": Care Leavers' Views of Preparing to Leave Care' – the executive summary includes the following.

» Many care leavers had no control over where they lived when they left care, and many felt unsafe.

» Although statutory guidance requires that young people should be introduced to their personal adviser (PA) from age 16, over a quarter of care leavers did not meet their PA until they were 18 or older.

» Many care leavers felt 'alone' or 'isolated' when they left care and did not know where to get help with their mental health or emotional well-being.

» More than a third of care leavers felt that they left care too early.

Feeling anxious comes naturally to me. I often wonder if it has stemmed from my childhood and if I will always be an anxious person. Being in care is like being stranded on an island, scared for your safety, worried about your future, wondering where you are going to end up but also knowing that there are 'treasure boxes' waiting for you, somewhere. You just need to find the courage and the motivation to explore the island, riding the waves through the unknown and unfortunately sometimes just going with the flow. Being in care is not a bad thing at all. I am so proud of my care leaver status. It has enabled me to do so many positive things in my life and hopefully will throughout the rest of my life. I have had opportunities that many young people do not get; however, this has only been since I have been older and have been involved with services. When I was younger I never wanted to accept any help and I would often miss appointments on purpose or just be a pain in general. It was not until I left school and became independent that I accepted more help from services such as the leaving care team.

I have met so many inspirational individuals throughout my journey and I have also met many people that are struggling and feel lost. Being a child in care is humiliating, frightening and soul destroying but with the right help and support from people who truly care it can make life that little bit easier.

It is so easy to judge, to make an assumption; however, it is even easier to listen. It takes no effort at all and could be the foundation to starting a positive future for others.

Dedication from Shannon

This chapter is dedicated to my Nan and Keith, who gave up their lives to be my kinship carers. Without their continued guidance and love through life, I would not be who I am today. You put your lives on hold for me for 18 years and I will forever be grateful; I owe you both the world. The constant support, love, dedication; the list is endless. To me, you are both my heroes.

In memory of Keith Standen 1945–2019.

I would like to say a massive thank you to Richard Williams for the constant support and encouragement throughout not only this chapter in this book but the three years that I have been a student at Bournemouth University. From the day of my interview, you have played a huge role in building me as a person and had a massive impact upon my learning and I will forever be grateful of that and to you.

And Mel Hughes, thank you for the opportunity of writing a chapter in your book and for your encouragement throughout this and my time at BU. Such an amazing opportunity that I would not have been able to do without you picking me as a suitable candidate so thank you.

Shannon.

References

Bergin, C and Bergin, D (2009) Attachment in the Classroom. *Educational Psychology Review*, 21: 141–70.

Bomber, L and Hughes, D (2013) *Settling Troubled Pupils to Learn: Why Relationships Matter in School.* London: Worth Publishing.

Children Act 1989 [online] Available at: www.legislation.gov.uk/ukpga/1989/41/contents (accessed 8 August 2022).

Children (Leaving Care) Act 2000 [online] Available at: www.legislation.gov.uk/ukpga/2000/35/contents (accessed 8 August 2022).

Children's Commissioner for England (2019) *Stability Index 2019: Overview Report.* [online] Available at: www.childrenscommissioner.gov.uk/report/stability-index-2019 (accessed 8 August 2022).

Department for Education (DfE) (2018) Extending Personal Adviser Support to All Care Leavers to Age 25: Statutory Guidance for Local Authorities. [online] Available at: https://assets.publishing.service.gov.uk/government/uploads/system/uploads/attachment_data/file/683701/Extending_Personal_Adviser_support_to_all_care_leavers_to_age_25.pdf (accessed 9 August 2022).

Department for Education (DfE) (2020) *Outcomes for Children Looked After by Local Authorities in England, 31 March 2019*. [online] Available at: https://assets.publishing.service.gov.uk/government/uploads/system/uploads/attachment_data/file/884758/CLA_Outcomes_Main_Text_2019.pdf (accessed 8 August 2022).

Downie, J and Twomey, B (2022) NYAS: My Things Matter, [online] Available at: https://nyas.s3.eu-west-1.amazonaws.com/NewsCampaigns/Campaigns/NYAS-My-Things-Matter%20(1).pdf (accessed 9 August 2022).

Farmer, E, Selwyn, J and Meakings, S (2013) 'Other Children Say You're Not Normal Because You Don't Live with Your Parents'. Children's Views of Living with Informal Kinship Carers: Social Networks, Stigma and Attachment to Carers. *Child & Family Social Work*, 18(1): 25–34.

Fearon, R, Bakermans-Kranenburg, M and Van IJzendoorn, M (2010) The Significance of Insecure Attachment and Disorganisation in the Development of Children's Externalising Behaviour: A Meta-Analysis. *Child Development*, 81: 435–56.

Glyde, T (2014) Wanting to be Normal. *The Lancet Psychiatry*, 1(3): 179–80. [online] Available at: www.thelancet.com/journals/lanpsy/article/PIIS2215-0366(14)70325-6/fulltext (accessed 8 August 2022).

Gorin, S, Baginsky, M, Moriarty, J and Manthorpe, J (2021) 'She Made You Feel like There's Hope': Gaining a Better Understanding of How Children Negotiate Their Relationships with Social Workers from Their Own Accounts. *British Journal of Social Work*, 51(8): 3135–52.

Jackson, S and Cameron, C (2012) Leaving Care: Looking Ahead and Aiming Higher. *Children and Youth Services Review*, 34(6): 1107–14.

Kincaid, S, Roberts, M and Kane, E (2019) Children of Prisoners: Fixing a Broken System. [online] Available at: www.nicco.org.uk/userfiles/downloads/5c90a6395f6d8-children-of-prisoners-full-report-web-version.pdf (accessed 9 August).

Marsden, H (2017) *Journey to Justice: Prioritising the Wellbeing of Children Involved in Criminal Justice Processes Relating to Sexual Exploitation and Abuse*. [online] Available at: www.basw.co.uk/system/files/resources/journey_to_justice_full_report_0.pdf (accessed 8 August 2022).

Office for National Statistics (ONS) (2022) Number and Percentage of Households with a Grandparent as Head of Household Living with Their Grandchildren, UK, 2006 to 2017. [online] Available at: www.ons.gov.uk/peoplepopulationandcommunity/birthsdeathsandmarriages/families/adhocs/009645numberandpercentageofhouseholdswithagrandparentasheadofhouseholdlivingwiththeirgrandchildrenuk2006to2017 (accessed 8 August 2022).

Ofsted (2022) 'Ready or not': care leavers' views of preparing to leave care. Gov.uk. [online] Available at: www.gov.uk/government/publications/ready-or-not-care-leavers-views-of-preparing-to-leave-care (accessed 14 September 2022).

Pritchard, C, Brown, K, Kleipoedszus, S and Williams, R (2018) *An International Perspective of Fostering and Adoption Outcomes: Developing an Evidence-Based Practice Policy*. Bournemouth: The National Centre for Post-Qualifying Social Work and Professional Practice, Bournemouth University.

Raikes, B (2016) 'Unsung Heroines': Celebrating the Care Provided by Grandmothers for Children with Parents in Prison. *Probation Journal*, 63(3): 320–30.

Romano, E, Babchishin, L, Marquis, R and Fréchette, S (2015) Childhood Maltreatment and Educational Outcomes. *Trauma, Violence & Abuse*, 16(4): 418–37.

Rubin, D M, Alessandrini, E A, Feudtner, C, Mandell, D S, Localio, A R and Hadley T (2004) Placement Stability and Mental Health Costs for Children in Foster Care. *Pediatrics*, 113(5): 1336–41.

Sattler, K, Font, S and Gershoff, E (2018) Age-specific Risk Factors Associated with Placement Instability Among Foster Children. *Child Abuse & Neglect*, 84: 157–69.

Chapter 4

Being transgender

Jay Alex Murray and Orlanda Harvey

My name is Jay, and I would like to tell you my story. I love sports; I used to play lacrosse and pool and I am a Formula 1 racing fan. I have a disability, I am an educator and I am a trans man.

I am passionate about sharing my experiences as there so are many trans people who don't have a voice and I hope that I can help by sharing my story. This is my story, with my opinions and experiences of being trans and may not reflect the experiences of all transgender people. When I sat down with Orlanda to work on this chapter, we quickly realised that it would be impossible to capture it in 4000 words, especially as I am still on a journey of discovery about myself and my identity – who I really am. Consequently, we drew up a timeline to capture the pivotal points in my life and explore each of these in turn. Inevitably my journey has been shaped by those around me and the society in which I live, so I am also going to share my thoughts about some of the wider social and political issues that have impacted on my life.

My story

I knew when I was five that I was different. I was assigned female gender at birth, but I'd always been a tomboy. I have a photo album that belonged to my grandparents, and there's about 12 photos of me in a dress or a skirt. They are nowhere else in the family albums just in formal pictures of events. When I was 12, I went to an all-girls' school. I realised I shouldn't be there; I couldn't be me, I couldn't relate, I was made to conform and never fitted in. My friends went down the make-up and fancy clothes path and I was like: what the hell are they doing putting on this blue eyeshadow rubbish? It wasn't for me. My mum got me some boots with a tiny heel on and they were so damn awkward, it was like: why are you making me wear these?

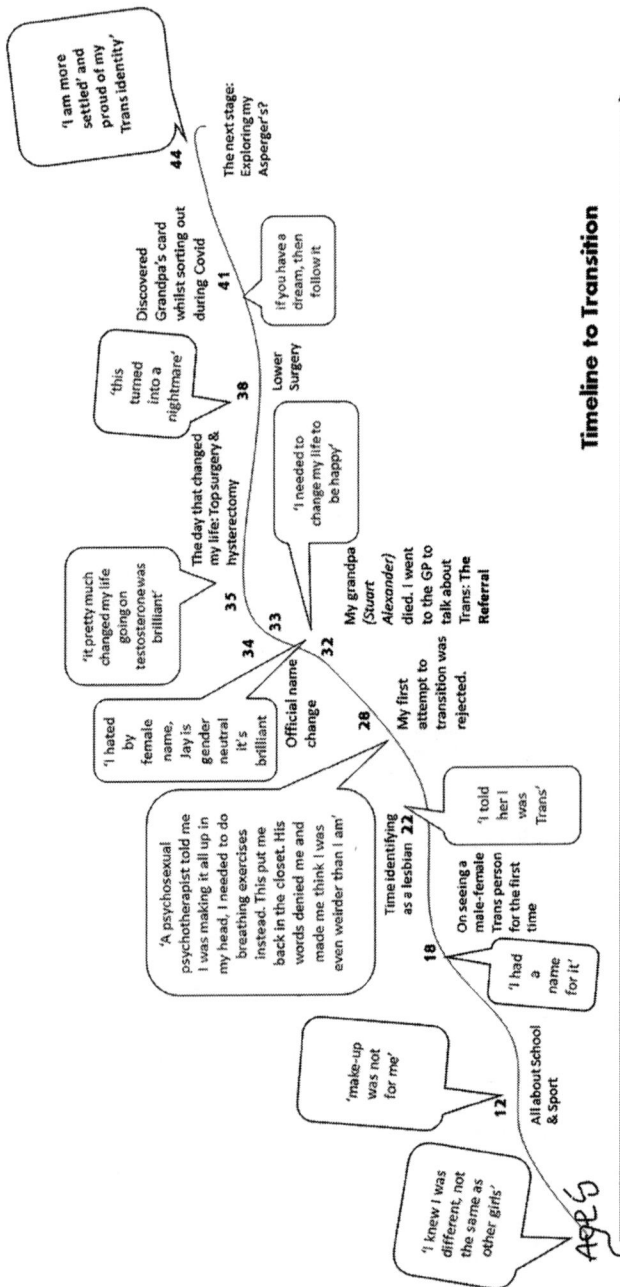

Figure 4.1 Timeline to transition

Reflective activity

Definition: *Trans*: An umbrella term to describe people whose gender is not the same as, or does not sit comfortably with, the sex they were assigned at birth (Stonewall, no date).

The UK government tentatively estimate that there are approximately 200,000–500,000 trans people in the UK (UK Government, 2021).

For trans men (transitioning from female to male), *'making the decision to change is influenced by a desire to achieve a sense of authenticity, since living in their birth sex trans men feel they are pretending to be someone they are not, trying to fit into the social roles expected of them'* (Atnas et al, 2015, p 39).

Take a moment here to reflect on your own sense of identity:

» How does it feel to be 'who you are'?

» Do you feel you 'fit in'?

» How might it feel to live a life where you cannot be your authentic self?

I was that sporty kid; I hid behind it. Every lunchtime I would spend the time hitting a ball against a wall. I loved archery and played lacrosse because it was an 'aggressive' sport and helped me to get some of the 'grrrr' out. Now, it makes sense because I was indirectly hiding from something I didn't know anything about. I was hiding from what didn't feel right and I liked sport because it did not reflect on my female character as such. I was in turmoil; I self-harmed and punched things.

When I was 18, I was seeing this guy (Jasper) and he told me to watch a programme that had a male to female trans person in it. Everything they were saying I understood, but from the opposite perspective, and it sort of gave me a name for it. I could so relate to that person. Despite this, Jasper and I went out for another year, even though he knew that I was kind of trans. It is different now for young people, as there is the terminology. When I was five or six, there was no transgender terminology anywhere.

Reflective activity

Section 28 of the Local Government Act was enacted in May 1988. It was brought in to *'prohibit the promotion of homosexuality by local authorities'*. This meant that discussion about identity and gender and sexuality was not allowed within schools. It was not repealed until 2003.

How do you think this might have impacted Jay's formative years?

When I was 22, I went down the lesbian route trying to conform, but it wasn't right at all. It wasn't right but I hid there for ten years, too scared to come out again. I used illicit drugs to try to fit in. I tried to come out at 28 but was sent to the wrong service: a psychosexual psychotherapist who was not qualified. He told me I was making it all up and to do breathing exercises! This put me back in the closet for four years. It was only when my grandpa passed away that I had the courage to be true to myself, with the realisation that only I can make me happy. Those words from the therapist denied me and still haunt me today. He was a sex therapist not a gender psychologist, so it was inappropriate to send me there.

During this period, I used to hang out with lesbians who wouldn't accept trans women in female spaces. I was watching their hatred.

I lost my grandpa when I was 32 and was sent to bereavement counselling. After the first session I was told I had underlying issues. I realised this was my time to stay as I am or be brave enough to transition. Soon after this, I went to my GP and spoke about being trans. He referred me to a local psychotherapist. I was meant to have six one-hour sessions of psychotherapy. I was in and out in 20 minutes with a referral to the gender clinic in London. They identified my needs, which was both amazing and scary at the same time, a big step into the unknown. I had blood tests and on 6 May (best day ever!) I started testosterone. I stopped taking illicit drugs at this time. On testosterone you're changing your body, everything changes, but you don't get any counselling for that. I was referred for my lower surgery. After this, I was discharged from the clinic. I was left with nowhere to go if I had further issues, only my poor GP who had little knowledge about transitioning. We teach GPs in essence, which is tough going.

Seeking initial support from a GP (general practitioner)

Jay's experience here has been echoed by others who wish to transition, as more than half (54 per cent) of trans people have reported that they have been told by their GP that they don't know enough about trans-related care to provide it (McNeil et al, 2012).

Atnas et al (2015) argue that health and support service commissioners, GPs and therapists need a great depth of knowledge and understanding to enable trans men better access to services. There are still people who are offered or pressured into undergoing conversion therapy and in the UK 5 per cent of LGBT people have been pressured to access services to question or change their sexual orientation when accessing healthcare services; this rises to 9 per cent of Black, Asian and minority ethnic LGBT people (Stonewall, 2018).

To physically transition, I was offered a bewildering range of procedures: bi-lateral mastectomy, reduction, mammoplasty, hysterectomy, salpingectomy, vaginectomy, oophorectomy, phalloplasty, urethroplasty, scrotoplasty with testicular protheses. My first operation was a bi-lateral mastectomy (removal of both breasts). I was not able to have a mastopexy (nipple replacement) as it is deemed cosmetic. They wouldn't fund the repositioning of my nipples as that was deemed cosmetic and not essential for a double mastectomy for trans men. I had to fight against the clinical commissioning group for my nips and won thankfully as funding comes from NHS England. I shouldn't have been put in that position to start with. I'm lucky I have a good chest, barely any scars so I'll take that one. I chose to have a hysterectomy, because I felt having a womb was part of a female identity. It was a horrible experience, but the combination of the two surgeries really chilled me out. It changed my life. I didn't have a mirror for years because I couldn't stand the way I looked. Now, I've got three or four.

After that, I had difficulty with my partner who was abusive, and there was no support for me. The lower surgery team made me wait an extra year before they would take me seriously because of what my partner was doing. My situation was so bad the police moved me out of where I was living. They tried to send me to Birmingham to a male refuge because it was the closest refuge to me. I did not want to move as I needed to be in the postal town for my referrals for my surgery and my birth certificate was female, so I thought I would be vulnerable in a male refuge.

It takes three major operations to construct a phallus and my first one lasted 11 hours. They took two strips of skin from my forearm plus an artery to provide feeling, and replaced it with flesh from my buttocks; they created an inbuilt urethra from hairless tissue and attached the new penis. This has left me with a large scar on my arm and nerve damage. Ironically, the scarring can be so specific that other trans people can identify me as a result – a type of 'transdar'. I also had a trans woman say that I had *'disfigured myself'*. The surgery hurt a lot, but I found I could deal with the pain as my head was in the right place. When I awoke from surgery, I felt a sense of peace. It was hard, because I had to go up to London without having anyone there with me, and then I had to get back to my hometown two hours away when I couldn't walk and I had a catheter. One time when I left hospital, they told me not to go near any schools or small children, as the bulge was padded and obvious.

I was meant to have three lower surgeries, but one did not go well. They put the wrong-sized implants in, and I have urethra issues. With the lower surgery, you get a pouch of water, a water reservoir in your tummy, you get one testicle and a pump, the implants go up the length of your phallus and then your ureter is in the middle. You have a choice as to whether you leave your clitoris where it is or have it removed. If you remove it you risk loss of sensation, but they can take a nerve out of your clitoris and thread it up your phallus, so in theory you'll get sensation and that has worked for me. I am getting less sensation now, so I'm worried about stuff, because I don't want to lose more sensation than I have. That's a real battle in my head right now. I'm not entirely sure I particularly like what I've got right now. Overall, for my transition from female to male I have had over 40 hours of surgery (although with my lower surgery, as it went wrong, I had eight operations) so far. Considering all the major surgery, no counselling is offered. I needed support at the time and had nothing.

In a way although I had an internal male identity I also had to learn 'how to be a man'. I looked up to one of my cis male friends, a six-foot-three mechanic. He was amazing and showed me what it was like to be a bloke without telling me, through his actions and how he was with people. He taught me a hell of a lot about men.

History

For many, the phenomenon of being trans seems very modern and 21st century. This is not the case.

Norman Haire (1892–1952) was a medical practitioner who carried out the first successful gender reassignment surgery (GRS) on Dora Richter, who underwent three procedures reassigning from male to female between 1922 and 1931 (Haire et al, 1968). In the UK, GRS was pioneered by Sir Harold Gillies.

Michael Dillon was educated at an exclusive girls' school and had been President of the Oxford Women's University Boat Club and a physician. Harold Gillies performed the first phalloplasty on him in 1946. In transitioning from female to male, Dillon underwent a total of 13 operations, over four years (Partridge, 2015).

Roberta Cowell, a married father of two, celebrated racing driver and Second World War fighter pilot was the first known British person to undergo male to female GRS. Michael Dillon operated illegally on Cowell as the operation was forbidden because it was considered 'disfiguring' of a man who was otherwise qualified to serve in the military. The operation helped Roberta obtain documents confirming that she was intersex and have her birth gender formally re-registered as female. Gillies performed a vaginoplasty on Roberta in 1951 (Blackstock, 2018).

My mum had breast cancer just before I came out, and that was tough because she needed a double mastectomy. She had all this going on, and I just sat there thinking how the hell am I ever going to explain it to her, because having breasts to me is part of womanhood. In a way the experience did me a favour because she didn't want me to get breast cancer. So, she was kind of cool with it, which was lovely because I expected it to be hard for her. My sister died when I was eight and I have always felt the pressure of being her only daughter. She has lost two daughters, in essence, but gained another son, which I don't necessarily think she wanted, but it is what it is. My brothers are pretty cool with it. My dad just doesn't mention it.

I officially changed my name when I was 33, as at my first Gender Identity Clinic appointment they wouldn't take me seriously until I changed my name in law. I had to relinquish my former name, so I was forced to tell my parents. Mum hated it and said she would continue to call me by my female name. It's so tough to pick your own name. I went through a few before I settled on Jay, which is gender neutral and perfect for me. I didn't want a really masculine name as I didn't know how I was going to turn out. My voice might have been one of the higher breaking voices; I may not have had a beard. Then I was sort of thinking about my mum and my dad, and Jay came from the initial of my sister. I thought this showed respect to my family. I think mum found that easier because it was not just a random name picked out but properly thought out. I do think it's helped her deal with it because I'm respecting the name she chose.

Mum even helped me to change my name a few days before my second appointment. The paperwork required for changing a name can be exhausting. For my passport I needed only a letter from the gender clinic and for my driving licence the deed poll showing my official name change. It was hard because now I had to deal with mum as well as dealing with the effects of starting treatment.

It was the beginning of this exciting part of my life, I'm lucky mum supported me but I also know she resented my transition as she'd lost a daughter. My transition was so hard to navigate because my mum is an emotional person. One time, we were at a restaurant celebrating mum's birthday and mum pointed in my direction using my female name. The waiter looked at me and was confused. I think that was when mum realised I was passing as male, and perhaps didn't like feeling stupid. After that she actively started to try and call me Jay. I don't take that personally because for 32 years I was her daughter. I still remember having to show my old ID and it was hard as I had a female ID and male presentation.

Reflective **activity**

Deadnaming is the term for using the former name of a trans and/or non-binary person without their consent.

When registering to vote the law requires you to declare your former names to be added to the electoral roll.

How might this be a barrier for trans people voting?

Reflecting on how far I have come, one moment that stands out is receiving a letter from my mother where she laid out her feelings about grieving for her daughter but embracing her son. It really showed me how much she cared about me, as she acknowledged my journey and helped me to understand the challenges for her as a parent. It helped me to feel accepted and supported:

I am not saying it's easy, it's not. It's bloody hard, but when you finish your journey, I just want you to know that we will love our son as much as we loved that lovely little girl we loved 34 years ago. I love you, and I'm sorry I get your name wrong sometimes.

(Extract from a letter to Jay from Jay's mum)

I've never had the conversation with either of my brothers. I think they are trying to get it but I don't think they understand; however, they don't judge me either. I think that's the important bit. My mum and dad were both psychiatric nurses and had come across trans people as far back as 1976, yet professional is different to personal. I believe that we're like the pebbles dropping in the water and we have to deal with every single ripple we create. You need every single person that surrounds you to go in with you, or without. If you can't be honest with your family, there are the knock-on effects from that.

It was not just my family life that was impacted. I was a top ladies pool player before I started my transition. The men I played pool with knew me as female and when I moved across to join the men's team, they sort of encouraged me when I wasn't quite good enough but when I started beating them, that's when they got funny with me. I found that I changed the way I played when I transitioned too. It could be that women might learn to play one way and men learn another way but when you're trans you have that neat unique experience of moving across, and therefore you learn both, so you can now do both. I thought I had been accepted and then I found out that one of the men outed me to another team in the league and that is technically illegal because it's a protected characteristic under the Equality Act 2010 and they're not allowed to out me under professional surroundings. I looked up the English Pool Association policy to see if they had any support but there was nothing, even though they have a duty of care to look after my identity. So, I decided to stop playing. I need to concentrate on wellness rather than getting upset by people not accepting me.

Reflective activity

Since the Gender Recognition Act 2004 came into force, 4910 trans people have been issued a Gender Recognition Certificate (GRC) to legally change their gender (Government Equalities Office, 2018). Trans people need to meet the requirements set out in the Act, which are:

» a medical diagnosis of gender dysphoria;

» a report from a medical professional detailing any medical treatment;

» proof of having lived for at least two years in their acquired gender through, for example, bank statements, payslips and a passport;

» a statutory declaration that they intend to live in the acquired gender until death;

» if married, the consent of their spouse;

» payment of a fee of £5;

» submission of this documentation to a panel, which the applicant does not meet in person.

Once in receipt of a GRC, their birth certificate can be changed – this is useful to do as many organisations do not recognise a R+GRC as a form of ID. All legal rights and responsibilities will correspond to the legally updated gender and it provides protection from organisations sharing information about a person's gender without consent.

Read the requirements above and reflect on the following questions:

» Are there any requirements that you feel might impinge on a person's human rights?

» How would you feel if you had to have your spouse's permission to change your gender?

» Just under 5000 people have applied for a GRC but the government's estimation is that the UK has between 200,000–500,000 trans people. What might account for the disparity in these figures?

After the medical transition

I have a beard and a deeper voice, but I still have stupid girly hips. Nowadays, I find it so much harder to cry. I only cry when I am at my lowest levels of testosterone, just before my injection is due. It's weird as I see things as more black and white and feel more logical. I didn't expect that change. No one sort of warns you about that; it's a subtle change which I didn't really think of. Does it mean that testosterone is stopping me from being emotional or is my headspace just moving away from being in a female form? Every nine weeks, I experience a kind of turnover. And that's hard because I've got to base my life on my injections or tablets. It's quite intimidating, knowing I will need drugs for the rest of my life. Not knowing what the NHS is doing is a massive stress because several years ago I looked up how much it costs, and it was like £82 an injection (every nine to ten weeks) and that's a lot of money that I don't have.

My journey: stigma and social exclusion

Before testosterone, I thought I was really male. Once I'd been on testosterone for a little while, I started noticing the changes and I realised that I wasn't really. I identify as male but in a way I'm both; I'm not either. I've got 32 years of being female and now I am 12 years of male or whatever. How could I not be both? Technically, I hate the label 'transexual'; I prefer 'transgender'. Language is complex and personal. I am trans. I have experienced stigma because I am trans, but I am also one of the lucky ones. Being trans does not mean I have the same experiences as everyone in the trans community. For example, life is very different for the generation coming through now. There is a different experience for trans men and trans women. As a female to male, I get passing privilege. This means when I walk down the street now you wouldn't be able to tell the female; a lot of trans women don't 'pass'. I am one of the unseen ones because I fit; I can bind my top down, not speak in a high voice and I'll pass as a young lad. I do not experience the derogatory insults that many trans women hear. For me though it hurts when the incorrect pronouns are used. One of the other things that stands out for me is that in clubs, some people will often touch me to see what type of 'junk' I have, which is uncomfortable and technically sexual assault.

I try not to get caught up with the negativity around the transgender debate in the media, as it is uneducated. There are those who have a perception that we are just deluded lesbians that get fooled by the patriarchy, thinking we believe that men are better than women and that life is easier as a man, if you were born cis male of course. Trans men are always playing catch up.

The debate can be soul destroying; it is unkind and fuels fear, and as a result often trans people do not report the abuse they receive.

Stigma and social exclusion

Several countries across the world still criminalise LGBT people; for example, in Nigeria and Saudi Arabia this includes the use of the death penalty. In 2018, 34 countries in Europe required a mental health diagnosis to determine whether a person is transgender and legally able to affirm their gender on official documents. The World Health Organization (2019) recommends that countries stop categorising gender identities as a mental illness. Thirteen countries in Europe require enforced sterilisation before a person can legally change their gender (TGEU, 2018).

The 2015 US Transgender Survey (USTS) (the largest known survey of transgender respondents) estimated prevalence of previous suicide attempts in the transgender population at 40 per cent (James et al, 2016). Trans people had a significantly higher prevalence of current self-harming behaviour than the non-trans group, with 19 per cent currently engaging in self-harm. This self-harm was significantly more prevalent among trans men than trans women (Davey et al, 2016).

More than four in five (83 per cent) English trans young people have experienced name-calling or verbal abuse; three in five (60 per cent) have experienced threats and intimidation; and more than a third (35 per cent) of trans young people have experienced physical assault. More than one in four (27 per cent) English trans young people have attempted suicide and nine in ten (89 per cent) have thought about it. Seventy-two per cent have self-harmed at least once (Harrington, 2014).

One in four trans people report having been discriminated against at work. More than two in five (44 per cent) trans people (EU) have never disclosed to anyone at work that they are trans (FRA: European Union Agency for Fundamental Rights, 2014).

Two in five (40 per cent) trans people (UK) adjust the way they dress because they fear discrimination or harassment. Two in five (UK) (41 per cent) trans people and three in ten non-binary people (31 per cent) have experienced a hate crime or incident because of their gender identity in the last 12 months (Stonewall, 2018).

Hines (2020) suggests that a trans-exclusionary politics of moral panic can support the dominance of the patriarchy and lead to oppression of those who are diverse, that is, not seeing themselves in terms of being defined by the binary terms male and female.

Reflective activity

As a reflective activity, we suggest you watch this short video https://vimeo.com/203887555 (Graf, 2017) and then consider these questions:

» Have you met anyone who identifies as trans?

» How are trans people represented in the media?

» What factors affect stigma and social exclusion?

» How might societal stigma impact the perspectives of family and friends?

» How might you reduce stigma and social exclusion?

One of the challenges we face being trans is that society is not set up to recognise, value and support people who do not fit into the binary roles of male or female. We live in a heteronormative culture and can often feel excluded. I often meet people who when they find out I am trans struggle to know how to interact with me as I do not easily fit into how they see the world. As soon as one mentions the word trans, people are scared and deny you that option as they don't know what to do with you. I have already shared how challenging it can be to access any support regarding being transgender. Other examples include my fight for the repositioning of my nipples, as this is deemed cosmetic, yet it is part of the surgery for a cis woman who has a mastectomy for health reasons and the basic acceptance of who I am now. I have also experienced challenges due to organisations not understanding my needs. It took nine years to get an outreach worker relating to having experienced domestic abuse. She left two weeks later, and they have passed me to a drop-in cis man centre. Cis men intimidate me. It is not the right environment for me; I need female interaction. This has left me feeling alone, abandoned and judged because of my trans status. There are more everyday challenges ranging from people mis-gendering you on purpose; using a toilet when out and about; to using changing rooms, leisure centres and swimming pools; to accessing services. Society is binary.

In essence, I now pass as male and have the male privilege that comes with that but, and it is a 'big but', as I was not brought up as male, my default is female. I went to an all-girls' school and tried to conform as female for 34 years pre-testosterone. I've never been taught how to be a man, how a man acts or what they believe. People talk to me differently now, and sometimes when they find out I am trans, people think it is their right to gossip about me. It's eye opening to witness the differences between the two binary genders and the extremes of both. Men talk to me on a totally different level; women do too. I believe a lot of people just presume I'm a gay cis man as apparently I am in touch with my feminine side, so I have been told. Nothing to do with my rainbow shoelaces ha-ha but I have to play on it a bit or I would slowly drive myself crazy thinking about what other people think of me. It has held me back so many years. Sometimes I get the flipside of that and get told – well, you wanted to be a man, you asked for all this. All what exactly? I just want to fit in, somewhere. This world currently isn't made for anyone outside of the binary. I am a human being, I have thoughts and emotions just like everyone else; why can't I be treated as such? Words hurt, a lot.

For me it is important that those who support us are non-judgemental, take the time to listen and find out who we are and learn about our experiences, rather than making assumptions or assigning a label. I do not mind if people make mistakes if they are willing to learn. Small changes might help people who are trans to feel less on the outside, such as forms being more inclusive with a few trans/non-binary options; that tiny change of wording would make so many of us feel more included in this world. For me the hardest thing is when people deliberately misgender me or are open in their transphobia. It is important for me to share my experiences with others to help them understand.

A great tool is the 'Genderbread person' (Killermann, 2017).

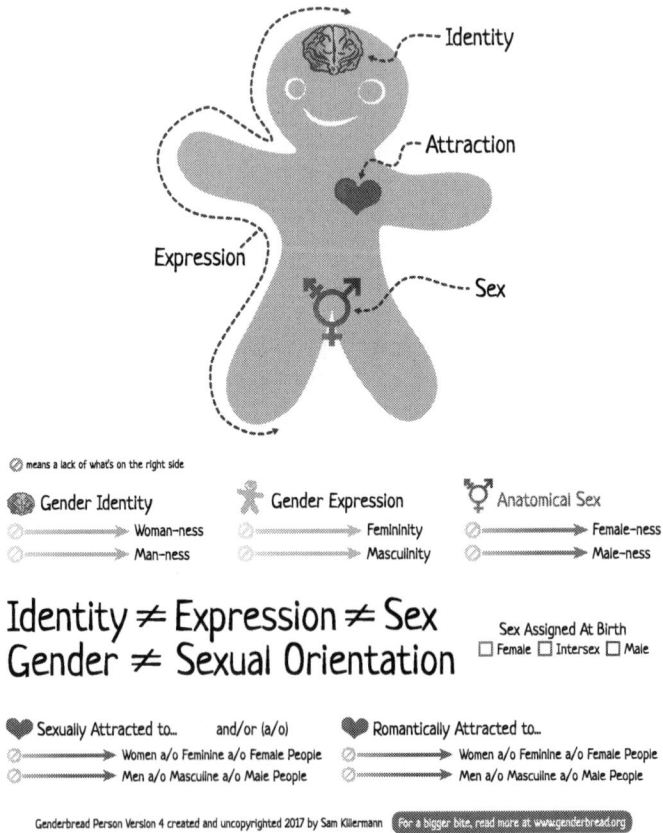

Figure 4.2 Genderbread person

People need to understand that gender is a social construct. All of us have got a bit of male and female and it just depends how much there is. We're all on the same spectrum so I think people should be able to tolerate all genders.

Reflective **activity**

Please watch these videos from a BBC documentary: *No More Boys and Girls – Can Our Kids Go Gender Free?* (Palmer, 2017)

Episode 1: www.youtube.com/watch?v=wN5R2LWhTrY

Episode 2: www.youtube.com/watch?v=cp9Z26YglrA&t=0s

How do they add to your understanding of sex and gender?

Who am I now?

My journey is far from over, and I am still hoping to get support for the effects of the domestic abuse I experienced, which is difficult as there are so few support services available. I also potentially want to explore my autism. There's quite a few trans people on the autistic spectrum, a higher proportion than cis people apparently (Greenberg et al, 2018).

I have a card from my grandpa; I found it a couple of years ago in my drawer, and that was quite a moment because I realised how far I had come. At the time I had been given it, I wouldn't have read any of the text; I would have gone '*oh, nice card*'. When I thought about it, I realised it was as if he knew before he passed away. It basically says:

If you have a dream, then follow it, when they come through, but it will only happen if you really want it to. You can't sit back and waste a minute, seize your chance today. Do what your heart is telling you, and let it lead the way I look to your style and follow it, and make your dream come true for who you are and where you go depends only on you.

I think he's looking down on me now being quite proud of me. I'm much more settled now.

Orlanda: Working with Jay to write this account of his life has been a joy and a privilege.

Language and terminology	
AFAB	Assigned female at birth
AMAB	Assigned male at birth
Cis or cisgender	Relating to a person whose sense of personal identity and gender corresponds with their birth sex.
Conversion therapy	Conversion therapy (or 'cure' therapy or reparative therapy) refers to any form of treatment or psychotherapy which aims to change/suppress a person's gender identity. It assumes that being lesbian, gay, bi or trans is a mental illness that can be 'cured'.

$\rightarrow$

Language and terminology	
Gender confirmation surgery (also called gender reassignment surgery)	Refers to doctor-supervised surgical interventions. Not all transgender people choose to, or can afford to, undergo medical surgeries.
Gender dysphoria	A sense of unease or distress that a person may feel because of a mismatch between their sex assigned at birth and their gender identity. Gender dysphoria can change over time. Not everyone who is non-binary or transgender experiences gender dysphoria.
Gender expression	A person's external presentation of their gender identity, which could include clothing, mannerisms and interests.
Gender Identity Clinic (GIC)	A service, which often includes a multi-disciplinary administrative and clinical team, including psychologists, psychiatrists, endocrinologists, speech and language therapists, and nurses. It provides holistic gender care, focusing on the biological/medical, psychological and social aspects of gender.
LGBTQ+	Lesbian, gay, bisexual, transgender, queer, questioning, plus came into regular usage in the 1990s.
Misgendering	Referring to someone using a word, usually a name or pronoun, that does not align with their gender.
Non-binary	An umbrella term to describe people whose gender is neither man or woman.
Transexual	Historically the term was used to indicate a difference between one's gender identity and sex assigned at birth. More specifically (although this is contentious), the term is often used when a person has undergone medical changes, such as hormones or surgery, that help alter their anatomy to align with their gender identity.
Transgender	Denoting or relating to a person whose sense of personal identity and gender does not correspond with their birth sex.
Transitioning	The steps a trans person may take to live authentically in line with their gender identity.
Transvestite	A person who dresses in clothes primarily associated with the opposite sex (typically used of a man).

References

Atnas, C, Milton, M and Archer, S (2015) Making the Decision to Change: The Experiences of Trans Men. *Counselling Psychology Review*, 30(1): 41–2.

Blackstock, E (2018) Fighter Pilot, Racing Driver, Prisoner of War, Transgender Pioneer: The Incredible Story of Roberta Cowell. *Jalopnik*. [online] Available at: https://jalopnik.com/fighter-pilot-racing-driver-and-prisoner-of-war-the-1828235092 (accessed 8 August 2022).

Davey, A, Arcelus, J, Meyer, C and Bouman, P (2016) Self-injury Among Trans Individuals and Matched Controls: Prevalence and Associated Factors. *Health and Social Care in the Community*, 24(4): 485–94.

FRA: European Union Agency for Fundamental Rights (2014) *European Union Lesbian, Gay, Bisexual and Transgender Survey – Main Results*. [online] Available at: https://doi.org/10.2811/37969 (accessed 8 August 2022).

Government Equalities Office (2018) *Trans People in the UK*. [online] Available at: https://assets.publish ing.service.gov.uk/government/uploads/system/uploads/attachment_data/file/721642/GEO-LGBT-factsheet.pdf (accessed 8 August 2022).

Graf, J (2017) Headspace. Vimeo. [online] Available at: https://vimeo.com/203887555 (accessed 8 August 2022).

Greenberg, D M, Warrier, V, Allison, C and Baron-Cohen, S (2018) Testing the Empathizing–Systemizing Theory of Sex Differences and the Extreme Male Brain Theory of Autism in Half a Million People. *Proceedings of the National Academy of Sciences of the United States of America*, 115(48): 12152–7.

Haire, N, Costler, A and Willy, A (1968) *Encyclopaedia of Sexual Knowledge*. London: Encyclopaedic Press.

Harrington, K (2014) *Youth Chances Survey of 16–25 Year Olds: First Reference Report*. Metro. [online] Available at: https://silo.tips/download/youth-chances-survey-of-year-olds-first-reference-report (accessed 8 August 2022).

Hines, S (2020) Sex Wars and (Trans) Gender Panics: Identity and Body Politics in Contemporary UK Feminism. *Sociological Review*, 68(4): 699–717.

James, S, Herman, J L, Rankin, S, Keisling, M, Mottet, L and Anafi, M (2016) *The Report of the 2015 US Transgender Survey*. Washington, DC: National Center for Transgender Equality. [online] Available at: www.transequality.org/sites/default/files/docs/USTS-Full-Report-FINAL.PDF (accessed 8 August 2022).

Killermann, S (2017) *Genderbread Person v4.0*. [online] Available at: www.genderbread.org/resource/gend erbread-person-v4-0 (accessed 8 August 2022).

Local Government Act 1988 [online] Available at: www.legislation.gov.uk/ukpga/1988/9/contents (accessed 8 August 2022).

McNeil, J, Bailey, L, Ellis, S, Morton, J and Regan, M (2012) *Trans Mental Health and Emotional Wellbeing Study 2012*. Scottish Transgender Alliance. [online] Available at: www.gires.org.uk/assets/Medpro-Assets/trans_mh_study.pdf (accessed 8 August 2022).

Palmer, S (2017) No More Boys and Girls: Can Our Kids Go Gender Free? BBC. [online] Available at: www. bbc.co.uk/programmes/b09202lp (accessed 8 August 2022).

Partridge, C (2015) Dillon, Michael (1915-1962). In *GLBTQ Literature* (pp 1–4). [online] Available at: www. glbtqarchive.com/literature/dillon_m_lit_L.pdf (accessed 8 August 2022).

Stonewall (2018) *LGBT in Britain: Trans Report*. [online] Available at: www.stonewall.org.uk/system/files/lgbt_in_britain_-_trans_report_final.pdf (accessed 8 August 2022).

Stonewall (nd) What Does Trans Mean? [online] Available at: www.stonewall.org.uk/what-does-trans-mean (accessed 8 August 2022).

TGEU (2018) *Trans Rights Europe Map & Index 2018*. [online] Available at: https://tgeu.org/trans-rights-europe-central-asia-index-maps-2020 (accessed 8 August 2022).

UK Government (2021) Trend Deck 2021: Demographics. [online] Available at: www.gov.uk/governm ent/publications/trend-deck-2021-demographics/trend-deck-2021-demographics (accessed 8 August 2022).

World Health Organisation (WHO) (2019) Gender Incongruence and Transgender Health in the ICD. [online] Available at: www.who.int/standards/classifications/frequently-asked-questions/gender-incon gruence-and-transgender-health-in-the-icd (accessed 9 August 2022).

Chapter 5 | Being a heroin and crack user

Phil, and Hannah Stott

My name is Phil, and in this chapter I will highlight my story with drug and alcohol use. I am 53 years old, originally from Hertfordshire and I love to do volunteer work and spend days at the beach during the summer months. I spend my free time reading and attending Cocaine Anonymous (CA) meetings.

I am sharing my story in the hope it will teach others about drug and alcohol use, and in doing so will highlight that, yes, we may have an addiction, but we are still human beings. I have been working alongside Hannah to think back over my life to put this chapter together to highlight my life outside of drug use; my life while engaged in drug use; and the long recovery I have been through to get to where I am today, which is nearly four years completely abstinent from any drugs and alcohol.

My drug and alcohol use story

My story starts when I was a child. My mother was a chronic alcoholic; she would always have a shelf full of all sorts of alcohol such as whiskey, gin and beer. This caused many arguments within my household between my parents, due to my mother coming back late after spending her evenings out drinking. I would hide away upstairs due to a fear of my parents. These arguments were only ever verbal; no physical harm was ever involved. However, at this point in my life I did experience sexual abuse. I would say my parents' relationship was quite dysfunctional. By this I mean I received no guidance or support, no love and no encouragement.

Parental alcohol or drug misuse in the UK

According to the Children's Commissioner for England's 2020 data on childhood vulnerability, there were 478,000 children living with a parent with problematic alcohol or drug use in 2019 to 2020. This is 1 in 25 children in the UK.

Impact of parental alcohol and/or drug misuse on children

The main implications of parental substance misuse for children can include a lack of support during puberty and early adolescence, increased psychological problems, conduct disorders and risk-taking behaviour (Cleaver et al, 1999, cited by Taylor et al, 2008). It can also lead to a failure to protect.

Parents are also often anxious to keep family matters hidden, leading to isolation and lack of support. Children may start to take a carer role and have problems at school, demonstrating difficult or worrying behaviour (Taylor et al, 2008).

My mother and father would have parties every Friday night. During one of these parties, when I was eight years old, I walked downstairs to go to the toilet and on the way started to pick up alcohol left around. At this point I had no idea what I was drinking and still to this day I'm not sure what I drank that night. The reason I carried on drinking during this night was that it made me feel warm and fuzzy, and overall took away the fear I had of my parents. This fear stemmed from the sexual abuse I experienced at this age and of my parents' anger. I believed that my father would hit me if I wasn't being quiet and doing as I was told. I thought that I might annoy people If I made too much noise. I used to try and make very little noise around the kitchen to ensure I wasn't noticed when I was making a cup of tea or getting a juice or an alcoholic drink. I would prefer to be outdoors as much as possible in wide-open spaces where I felt safe in comparison to when I was at home. I would try and sneak past my father's bedroom if the door was open because I believed and convinced myself that he wasn't asleep and that I could be in danger from him. He may have been asleep, but I wasn't going to take any chances. I believe this is the reason I continued to drink, to numb this fear and escape from it.

Reflective activity

Take a moment to think about what it is like to be eight years old.

» Can you think back to your own childhood and being eight? Do you know any children who are this age now?

» How would you describe a happy and safe life for an eight year-old child?

» How does this compare to what Phil describes here?

» What impact do you think it will have had on Phil and other children who are living in fear and don't feel safe at home?

My drinking continued from then on, from having a couple of mouthfuls before school until I was 16, to leaving school and starting to earn money, enabling me to buy this alcohol myself and therefore to start drinking a lot more, and more frequently. At this time of my life, all I was focused on was drinking and working. I had hobbies such as football and a large social life, but my mind always came back to work to gain the funds for alcohol. I became caught up in the obsession with drinking rather than the habit of drinking.

Prevalence of alcohol consumption in children

The Smoking, Drinking and Drug Use Among Young People in England survey in 2018 shows that 56 per cent of children aged 11–15 had never had an alcoholic drink.

The prevalence of children drinking alcohol increases sharply with age.

» 2 per cent of 11 year olds of either gender reported drinking alcohol in the past week.

» 21 per cent of males and 24 per cent of females aged 15 years old reported drinking in the past week.

Children who had drank in the last week were most likely to have done so on Saturday (67 per cent), followed by Friday (38 per cent) and then Sunday (30 per cent). The proportion for weekdays was 10 per cent or less (Zambon, 2021).

Type of alcohol consumed by young people					
	Beer/Cider	Shandy	Wines	Spirits	Alcopops
Boys	87%	19%	27%	52%	27%
Girls	65%	13%	55%	67%	39%

In a national household survey of adverse childhood experiences (ACEs) and their relationship with resilience to health-harming behaviours in England, Bellis et al (2014) found those who had experienced four or more adversities in their childhood were two times more likely to binge drink and 11 times more likely to use crack cocaine or heroin in the future (Bellis et al, 2014).

Smoking, heavy drinking and cannabis use in adulthood also increase with the number of ACEs that person has experienced (Aynsley et al, 2017).

At age 28, I started a family. My partner ended up being like a mother figure to me and we had two children together. I loved my family; however, I could never bond with them properly because I have had no one to learn from and look up to. Home life bored me. I always had to be out; my head was always focused on drinking. My partner and I split up after seven years of being together, but we managed to maintain a good relationship. She always allowed me open access to maintain a relationship with my children.

This was my life until I went into rehab at age 35 for six months. This rehab was for alcohol or heroin use, therefore introducing me for the first time to heroin. After coming out of rehab, I managed to stay abstinent for a further eight months. I then relapsed on alcohol and heroin. This is where my journey of taking drugs as well as alcohol started.

I ended up back in rehab after 18 months of drinking and using heroin. This ended my alcohol use, but the heroin use continued. I thought going to my GP for advice would help with this; however, this only resulted in me being given a methadone script. Methadone became my new addiction alongside heroin use for seven years. I really believed I could get high on methadone; however, in reality, it did nothing apart from stopping me from feeling physically ill. This sense of nothingness it gave me encouraged me to reduce the amount I was taking and eventually, in 2008, I ended up in Essex for a two-week detox from methadone.

Examples of treatment options

Detoxification programmes (detox)

Detox services are designed to deal with the effects of alcohol and drugs and the potential for physical withdrawal symptoms, typically through the use of prescribed medications.

Detox programmes typically offer a three to five-day stay during which the client is medically withdrawn from the drugs and alcohol to avoid physical withdrawal and, in extreme cases, delirium tremens known as DTs or the shakes (Mignon, 2014).

Methadone maintenance treatment (MMT)

Methadone maintenance has been used to treat opioid dependence since the 1950s. Methadone is taken in daily doses as a liquid or pill in order to reduce withdrawal symptoms and cravings for opioids. Methadone is addictive but it is safer for the patient to take this under medical supervision compared to opioids of an unknown purity (World Health Organization, 2009).

Rehabilitation (rehab)

Rehab provides the client with a break from work and family responsibilities and allows complete focus on recovery. It provides a higher level of medical supervision than is available in the community and can help patients to increase awareness of the trigger or triggers that place them at risk of relapse (Weiss, 1994, cited by Mignon, 2014).

Rehabilitation programmes are typically 30 days, 60 days or 90 days in duration but can be longer, often depending on funding and the services available.

Upon leaving this residential detox, I relapsed and started using heroin again. I also started using crack cocaine. I believe my relapse happened due to having a brutal and harsh detox. I was on 25ml of methadone when I went into the detox unit. I reduced and detoxed by using Subutex (a tablet which is used to prevent withdrawal symptoms), which was horrible. The withdrawals and insomnia were torture and exhausting. After four months of not sleeping, feeling restless and irritable, I decided to use heroin. I couldn't see any other solution to my ongoing problem of insomnia and mental torture. I chose this option with a clear head, and at the time nobody was going to stop me.

I enjoyed using heroin as it felt comforting and 'like a cure'. This led to me becoming addicted enough to start injecting and this became the new normal for me. I continued using heroin and crack cocaine for years. It felt nice and at this time I was in complete denial that I was addicted, and therefore I kept increasing the usage amount over these years. I spent a lot of time with other heroin and crack users. We all lived in the same housing estate, meaning I was unable to escape it.

At this point in my life, I was so blind to my addiction that it took over me. I was on benefits and would use it all up in one day on drugs to the point where I couldn't even afford to pay the extra £12 a month it would cost to top up my rent. I would have to go to food banks or shoplift to eat. This was a cycle every two weeks. It progressively got worse, so I had to earn money by running drugs around for other people. I put drugs in front of everything else and became blind to other things going on in my life.

Different theoretical models to help understand substance use

Medical model of substance use

Addiction, *addict*, *alcoholism* and *alcoholic* are terms typically based on biological or medical models of substance use. They focus on the physical dependence and withdrawal from substances and view substance dependence as a disease or illness.

Walters and Rogers (2011) explain how biomedical consequences can explain how 'alcoholism' and other drug 'addictions' are diseases such as the dangerous withdrawal symptoms individuals with a physical dependence may face. Alongside this, cardiac conditions, hypertension or liver and pancreatic diseases may also require treatment. The medical consequences model acknowledges how alcohol and drug use leads to a variety of medical, psychological and social consequences. The distress these consequences cause leads to further substance misuse, leading to more consequences. Walters and Rogers (2011) explain how this can form a vicious cycle.

Another model is one that takes into account physical dependence but also acknowledges the psychological and social *causes* as well as *consequences*.

Bio-psycho-social model of substance use

The bio-psycho-social model of substance use is more widely accepted in social work settings. It is based on the principle that genetic, personality, psychological, social and cultural factors must be considered when seeking to understand both the *causes of* and *consequences of* problematic substance use. In social work we aim to avoid terms which label the person, such as *addict* and *alcoholic*, and focus on terms that focus on the behaviour without attributing blame, such as *substance user*. This is particularly relevant to a discussion on social exclusion and the impact of stigma and discrimination on a substance user's relationship with wider society.

Interventions based on this model incorporate strategies to enhance coping, reduce cravings and manage triggers to prevent relapse (Skewes and Gonzalez, 2013) but also seek to understand the root causes of the substance use such as adverse childhood experiences (ACEs). Support based on this model helps people manage their emotions to cope with negative life events and enhances social support for sobriety or a reduction in use. Typically, the course of action to aid recovery is led by the person themselves.

The 12-step approach to recovery such as Alcoholics Anonymous (AA) or Cocaine Anonymous (CA) is based on a bio-psycho-social-spiritual model of addiction (Walters and Rogers, 2011). It is rooted in a medical dependence model and advocates the need for complete sobriety. This is the support option that has worked well for Phil.

Understanding problematic substance use and dependent behaviour

UK Rehab describes six stages of 'addiction'.

1. Experimentation: Habits tend to start with experimenting. It often starts with curiosity about a particular substance or activity and the individual tries it to see if they find it enjoyable.
2. Desire: If the individual tries something and enjoys it, this sense of enjoyment leads to a desire for it. However, at this stage, the individual isn't actively seeking it out.
3. Want: When desire occurs more often, it becomes a want. The individual will plan ahead and do whatever they have to ensure their desire is satisfied.
4. Habit: When the want becomes more frequent, a habit has been formed. At this stage, the individual will engage in an activity without actually thinking about it.
5. Need: At this stage, the individual may start to feel like they can't do without a drink or drug. They also surrender control.
6. Addiction: Once control has been given to a substance, addiction has developed. The person is now at a stage where they cannot quit even if they want to.

(UK Rehab, 2019)

Cycle of Change Model

The Cycle of Change Model is useful for understanding behavioural change. In the UK it frequently informs substance use work and has been used in other areas, such as supporting people experiencing domestic violence and abuse. The cycle was developed by Prochaska and DiClemente in the 1980s and aims to gauge people's readiness to make changes in their own lives. It acknowledges that change occurs best when it is genuinely desired rather than forced. This model shows the significant changes individuals go through and provides a framework for workers to understand these behavioural changes (Prochaska and DiClemente, 1986). The cycle of change model identifies the following stages: pre-contemplation (no intention of changing behaviour); contemplation (aware of problem but with no plans to address it); preparation (intent on taking action); Action (changing behaviour); maintenance (sustained period of change); and relapse (falling back into old behaviours (Prochaska and DiClemente, 1986)

Reflective activity

» Have you ever made a New Year's resolution and then found it difficult to stick to?

» Take a moment to think about a positive change that you have tried to make in your own life. It could be to go to the gym; stick to a diet plan; spend less time on social media. Choose an example and then use the cycle of change stages to help you think through your habits in making and maintaining this change.

» What helps and what doesn't?

During this time of my life, I went into residential detoxes and rehab centres but continued to relapse when leaving these. Until one day, in 2018, the drug project in my home county suggested I move down to the south coast and escape this area and the place I had always used drugs. I took this opportunity and went straight into detox for five months. On coming out I attended a structured day programme five days a week for relapse prevention.

From this day, I have never looked back. I have been completely abstinent from all drugs and alcohol for nearly four years. My recovery was tough and took multiple detoxes, multiple rehabs and many years but I got there. I am now strong enough to stay there. One thing I've maintained throughout my using and recovery was attending Alcoholics Anonymous, Cocaine Anonymous and Narcotics Anonymous meetings. I still attend these occasionally to this day. These groups have encouraged me to share my story and learn that I'm not alone in recovery by listening to other stories.

My journey with stigma due to my addiction

The term *druggie*

During my life, I have used many drugs, including heroin, crack, cannabis, ecstasy and speed. When using these, I would get angry and be in constant denial that I was a 'druggie'. I have been called many things during my life such as scumbag, loser and 'dirty'. One dehumanising term, however, is *druggie*. This term has made me feel judged and misunderstood. In the past, I would become extremely defensive when called this and I'd feel stripped of my self-esteem and self-confidence. This led my mental health to decline when I was around the age of 22. I suffered severely from depression and paranoia. I partly blame my cannabis use for this; however, constant name-calling and being judged rather than supported or helped for my actions also played a part.

Dual diagnosis

Many individuals diagnosed with a substance use disorder (SUD) also experience a co-occurring mental or behavioural condition. This is known as a dual diagnosis (Juergens, 2022).

Those with a dual diagnosis are often unable to access the care they need. Often mental health services exclude people due to co-occurring alcohol/drug use. Those with serious mental health illnesses may also be excluded from alcohol and drug services due to the severity of their mental illness (Christie, 2022).

There are several reasons why there is an unmet need for those experiencing dual diagnosis. It is down to both strategic and operational issues.

Strategic issues	Operational issues
• Services may fail to recognise that people's difficulties are not purely health related but are influenced by a range of other factors and practitioners may not be trained to address these. This can be an issue for individuals with a dual diagnosis as they require a range of interventions suited to their needs which no one treatment service or agency can meet. • There is a lack of designated dual diagnosis funding. A reason for this is due to funding being provided through a variety of routes. Since 2002 in England and Wales, funding has primarily focused on substance misuse, whereas dual diagnosis services are funded through Primary Care Trusts (PCTs).	• There is no universally agreed definition for dual diagnosis due to the differing needs of those experiencing it. It is also complex to define due to the underlying philosophy, eg the extent to which health and social models are adopted (Watson and Hawkings, 2002). • Developing effective partnerships can be difficult due to perceived hierarchies within professions and differing professional values, which may lead to competing priorities. Those working with individuals with a dual diagnosis often feel disempowered to develop partnerships due to not feeling listened to.

Today, when I am referred to as a druggie, I am ashamed of my past and feel a huge sense of guilt and remorse for my actions. I am embarrassed that this was how I chose to live my life previously.

How I believe people view drug users

There are many stigmas associated with drug or alcohol users, some of which can be true, and some which aren't. It is also believed that all drug users are the same; however, we are unique and have our own stories and journeys to share. Firstly, it is assumed that all drug or alcohol users rob older people, women in particular. When I was using, I would occasionally take food or other things from shops so I understand the view that drug users can be viewed as thieves. However, I personally have not stolen from an older person. I do believe what I did is a misdemeanour (a minor wrongdoing).

Drug crime rates in England and Wales

In 2020/21, there were around 210,000 drug offences recorded by the police. This is a 19 per cent increase from 2019/20. The number of arrests for drug offences peaked in 2010/11 at a rate of 119,000. This rate has since fallen to 69,000 in 2019/20.

Merseyside's recorded drug offences were the highest of around 9.2 per 1,000 population in 2020/21, which is an increase from 8.3 per 1,000 in 2019/20. Staffordshire had the lowest rate of drug offences with 1.4 per 1,000.

In 2018/19, there were around 48,800 cases dealt with for drug offences. Between 2008/09 and 2018/19, the proportion of drug offenders receiving a caution fell from 46 per cent to 30 per cent. However, during this period of time, the percentage of drug offenders sentenced increased from 9 per cent to 16 per cent (Allen and Tunnicliffe, 2021).

The Office for National Statistics found that between 2019/20 and 2020/21, the total number of drug offences increased by 19.3 per cent.

There was an increase in the recording of other drug offences over this period.

» Trafficking in controlled drugs increased by 32.9 per cent.

» Possession of controlled drugs increased by 16.3 per cent.

» Possession of cannabis increased by 21.5 per cent.

» Other drug offences increased by 38.25 per cent.

(Elkin, 2021)

Secondly, there is a strong belief that heroin and crack cocaine users are criminals and unemployable people compared to those who do not use drugs, due to these being class A drugs. They believe there is a class difference between those that use and those that don't, as they aren't taking the drugs. Being a heroin addict is also strongly associated with having HIV or AIDS. In some cases, this is true, but this is not true for most heroin users.

It is believed by many people that drug users could just stop using drugs if they really wanted to but wanting to stop isn't enough for addicts. I told myself throughout my journey many times that I would stop using and I meant it when I said it, but it was difficult to escape the habit.

Times I have been treated differently

When I was working, during the time I was using drugs it would be common for colleagues to take time off here and there due to being sick. I felt, however, that if I ever asked for a day off due to feeling ill, it would never go down well with management. I felt that due to my drug use I wasn't trusted. They would assume that the reason I asked for this time off was due to my drug use rather than due to illness. Whenever someone else took days off, it was never a problem and they would never be questioned.

Another time was when I was in shared housing, I wouldn't be invited to get-togethers due to my alcohol and drug use. They would think I was just going to get too drunk or high. I really felt judged and misunderstood as people didn't know my history or my story. Even now I am drug free, I feel if I were to apply for a job in the future, I wouldn't be offered the position due to my past addictions compared to someone who has never had these addictions. If I were to go to the doctors, I feel I wouldn't receive the same level of help as those who are non-addicts. This often leads me to feel like a 'social misfit'.

My views of different drugs				
• Prescription drugs are viewed as 'clean'.	• Crack and heroin are seen as dirty drugs, often associated with HIV, Hepatitis C and AIDS.	• Ecstasy is seen as a party drug and doesn't shock people when used.	• Cannabis is seen more as a harmless drug; more people accept its use and want to legalise it.	• Alcohol is related more to violence. It is seen as socially acceptable and safe to a lot of people.

My life now

When I first moved to the south coast, I went straight into a detox followed by rehab for five months until I lived where I live now. I have lived for three and a half years in supported housing with others who are also recovering addicts. This can be hard for me if they relapse, but I get through it; however, I do feel lucky as I live somewhere that is safe and clean.

In my free time, I complete a lot of volunteer work every week. I do two days volunteering at my supported housing and two days helping out an older woman gardening and doing little jobs for her. Other than this, I have a handful of close friends whom I trust and spend time with. I speak to my children and family regularly. I also try to make sure I attend CA meetings weekly.

Moving away was the right decision for me, although to start with I doubted this decision and questioned what I had done. I am happy with my decision and have turned my life around completely. Since living here, my mindset and I have changed, and I now feel like I can walk around with my head held high, proud of the person I am today and proud of how I have chosen to change my life for the better.

Recommended reading and viewing

The Anonymous People

> » This is a documentary film about 23 million individuals in the United States recovering from alcohol and drug addiction. It tells true stories of these people wishing to overcome the challenges of recovery.

That Sober Guy Podcast

> » This is hosted by a recovering addict who interviews a mix of celebrity guests or everyday people who have experienced addiction in their lives and share the impact this had on their lives. It can be accessed at: https://thatsoberguy.libsyn.com/

Society for the Study of Addiction

> » This website shows the latest findings around substance misuse and aims to broaden and promote the scientific understanding of addiction. It can be accessed at: www.addiction-ssa.org/

References

Alcoholics Anonymous (2021) About AA. [online] Available at: www.alcoholics-anonymous.org.uk/About-AA (accessed 8 August 2022).

Allen, G and Tunnicliffe, R (2021) *Drug Crime: Statistics for England and Wales*. House of Commons Library. [online] Available at: https://researchbriefings.files.parliament.uk/documents/CBP-9039/CBP-9039.pdf (accessed 8 August 2022).

Aynsley, A, Bradley, R, Buchanan, L, Burrows, N and Bush, M (2017) *Childhood Adversity, Substance Misuse and Young People's Mental Health*. Bournemouth: Addaction. [online] Available at: www.wearewithyou.org.uk/documents/6/young_minds_addaction_briefing_july_2017_web_0.pdf (accessed 8 August 2022).

Bellis, M A, Hughes, K, Leckenby, N, Perkins, C and Lowey, H (2014) National Household Survey of Adverse Childhood Experiences and Their Relationship with Resilience to Health-Harming Behaviours in England. *BMC Medicine*, 12(72).

Children's Commissioner (2020) CHLDRN – Local and National Data on Childhood Vulnerability. [online] Available at: www.childrenscommissioner.gov.uk/chldrn (accessed 8 August 2022).

Christie, E (2022) *Better Care for People with Co-occurring Mental Health and Alcohol/Drug Conditions*. London: Public Health England. [online] Available at: https://assets.publishing.service.gov.uk/governm ent/uploads/system/uploads/attachment_data/file/625809/Co-occurring_mental_health_and_alco hol_drug_use_conditions.pdf (accessed 8 August 2022).

Cocaine Anonymous (2021) *Cocaine Anonymous Cauk Area*. Tradition 6. [online] Available at: www. cocaineanonymous.org.uk (accessed 8 August 2022).

Elkin, M (2021) Crime in England and Wales: Appendix Tables. Office for National Statistics. [online] Available at: www.ons.gov.uk/peoplepopulationandcommunity/crimeandjustice/datasets/crimeinenglan dandwalesappendixtables (accessed 8 August 2022).

Jeurgens, J (2022) Dual Diagnosis. Addiction Center. [online] Available at: www.addictioncenter.com/addict ion/dual-diagnosis (accessed 8 August 2022).

Mignon, S I (2014) *Substance Abuse Treatment: Options, Challenges, and Effectiveness*. New York: Springer Publishing Company.

Narcotics Anonymous UK (2021) About Narcotics Anonymous. UKNA. [online] Available at: www.ukna.info (accessed 8 August 2022).

Prochaska, J O and DiClemente, C C (1986) Toward a Comprehensive Model of Change. In Miller, W R and Heather, N (eds) *Treating Addictive Behaviors*. Applied Clinical Psychology, vol 13. Boston, MA: Springer. https://doi.org/10.1007/978-1-4613-2191-0_1

Skewes, M C and Gonzalez, V M (2013) The Biopsychosocial Model of Addiction. *Principles of Addiction*, 1: 61–70.

Taylor, A, Toner, P, Templeton, L and Velleman, R (2008) Parental Alcohol Misuse in Complex Families: The Implications for Engagement. *British Journal of Social Work*, 38: 843–64.

UK Rehab (2019) The Stages of Addiction. [online] Available at: www.uk-rehab.com/addiction/the-stages-of-addiction (accessed 8 August 2022).

Walters, S T and Rotgers, F (2011) *Treating Substance Abuse: Theory and Technique*. 3rd ed. New York: Guilford Press.

Watson, S and Hawkings, C (2002) *Dual Diagnosis Good Practice Handbook*. London: Turning Point.

World Health Organization (2009) *Training Manual for Clinical Guidelines for Withdrawal Management and Treatment of Drug Dependence in Closed Settings*. Manila: WHO Regional Office for the Western Pacific.

Zambon, N P (2021) *Alcohol Statistics: England*. House of Commons Library. [online] Available at: https:// researchbriefings.files.parliament.uk/documents/CBP-7626/CBP-7626.pdf (accessed 8 August 2022).

Chapter 6 | Being a refugee

Ahed Al Hamwi and Rachael Sawers

My name is Ahed Al Hamwi. I am 41 years old. I am originally from Syria, which was a wonderful country before the 2011 war. I have two children: Anas is 16 years old and Amjad is 14 years old.

I studied English Language and Literature at Damascus University and I got my Bachelor's degree in 2003. In 2003, I also started teaching English as a second language; first in primary schools, then in secondary schools and after that I became a headteacher in a secondary school in Damascus (the capital of Syria), but I had to leave my job and my country because of the war.

Everything was good before the war. Syria was a beautiful, prosperous and peaceful country. Most people could manage to live comfortably on their salary. For me, I could buy a small flat near Damascus. Unfortunately, I was only able to live in it for just six months. I had to leave it when the tanks came to our area and started shooting the houses and the area randomly. I can still remember the day when we woke up early at about 6am hearing the helicopters hovering and bombing the area. At the beginning we went to the basement as it was safer than the flat. We stayed there until about 12pm when the tanks attacked the area. A lot of people were in the basement; the children were crying, while most of the men were going upstairs frequently to find out what was happening outside. After a while they said it was dangerous to stay in the basement as the tanks were getting closer and closer. Then, people started to run away with their children. My husband and I did the same; we carried our children and started running to the countryside where we could stay with a family. We hadn't met them previously, but they knew that our area was being bombed and they let us stay with them. They were very generous. They offered us food and drinks because we had left our houses without taking anything – we couldn't even take any money. We stayed with this family overnight while we were still hearing the tanks and the helicopters bombing our city far away the whole night. The sounds of missiles stopped in the morning, so we left that family and tried to go back to our area, but army personnel didn't let us go back. They said the area had been destroyed and that we should forget about going back to our houses. The only thing that we could do is to walk with the children to the countryside again and to find a way to go to my parents' flat in Damascus (about 11km away). The checkpoints were everywhere, and they prevented us from taking certain paths. At the beginning it seemed impossible to leave that place until finally while were walking, we met a taxi driver who said that he knew a safe way to go to Damascus. Although it was a very long journey through the countryside we did manage to get to my parents' flat eventually.

Reflective activity

Put yourself in the shoes of Ahed and her family. Imagine you are trapped in your building with the sound of tanks and bombing getting closer and closer. It is too dangerous to stay but there is no safe way to escape. What do you do? Stay or leave?

If you had to leave with no notice, without being able to return to your flat or home, what would you have to leave behind? What would you miss most? What impact would this have?

As you can see, we left suddenly, and we couldn't have known that it would be the last time we would see our flat. I still cannot understand why that terrible war started. All that we know is that in March 2011, 15 teenagers were arrested and brutally tortured by security forces for scrawling anti-government graffiti in the city of Daraa in the south of Syria (Macleod, 2011). Their inhumane arrests sparked peaceful civilian protests in the city. Some people from the city met with some people from the administration to calm the situation, but it was in vain. The anger escalated in a few days. Protestors demanded the end of corruption and chanted about their deep-rooted dissatisfaction towards the Assad regime. In response to the civilian uprising, government forces resorted to lethal violence and opened fire on unarmed protestors. On 25 April 2011, Daraa was besieged by the Syrian military. All incoming telephone lines, media, food and medicine supplies were blocked as forces exerted excessive and indiscriminate violence on civilians. This led to huge resentment against the government. Protests demanding the resignation of Bashar al-Assad – peaceful and disruptive alike – spread throughout Syria. It was not long before the country was embroiled in a civil war (BBC Radio 4, 2016).

The war turned the beautiful country into a large cemetery that accommodated thousands of dead people. The smell of death spread everywhere. My husband and I were worried about our children, so my husband decided to leave the country to find a safer place for us.

He left the country in June 2015. He went to Turkey first but as they do not give refugee status to people fleeing from war, he changed his direction to the UK and he started his long journey through the sea from Turkey to Greece, Macedonia, Serbia, Hungary and then he went through the forests to Austria. After that he went to Germany and then

France until he reached his destination in the UK in November 2015. The journey took him about five months, and it was a very difficult journey. He spent these days and nights in the forests and in camps while moving from one country to another until he arrived in the UK where, after getting refugee status, he applied for a family reunion visa. I then arrived in the UK with my boys in 2016. Although our journey was safer than his, I went through many challenging times with the boys in Syria during that year. There were a few months when my husband could not be in touch with us as he was in the forests, and I was very worried about him and about the boys.

Numbers

As of 2020, there are 6,568,000 internally displaced people in Syria (Statista.com, 2022). This is half of the entire Syrian population. Many Syrians have fled the country. In most cases, this was to Turkey (3,685,839), Lebanon (851,718), Jordan (668,332), Germany (616,325) and Iraq (345,952) (Statista.com, 2022).

According to ReliefWeb, one in three schools in Syria are in ruins or have been commandeered by armed groups and around 60 per cent of Syrians who remain lack access to safe, nutritious food.

In response, the UK set up the Syrian Vulnerable Persons Scheme with a target for 20,000 individuals to be resettled in the UK between 2015 and 2020. The target was met in early 2021 having been impacted by the Covid pandemic.

According to United Nations Refugee Agency (UNHCR), as of mid-2021 there were 135,912 refugees, 83,489 pending asylum cases and 3,968 stateless persons in the UK (UNHCR, 2021).

During this time, there were a lot of thoughts fighting in my head. I was thinking about things like: *'Am I going to be accepted by the British people? How will they treat us when we arrive? Are they going to accept us as Muslims and refugees?'* Of course, the media in Syria plays a crucial role in giving us the wrong impression. They portrayed that Western people hate Arabs and they don't want Muslims to live with them. I have heard many stories like that on TV and I have seen some short videos about people insulting Muslims, particularly those women who wear a hijab (the scarf which covers the hair). I remember seeing a short video in which a lady was walking with her little children when a man came from behind and hit her, pushed her to the ground and tried to remove her hijab. But there was no other choice – we had to leave the country.

It was not an easy choice for me to leave Syria. It meant leaving my parents, my job, my friends and even my flat, which was bombed, but it was the cruelty of war which pushed us to find a safer place and a better future for our children. This is the most important thing for me.

When I arrived in the UK, the first person I met was a lady from the Red Cross who had helped my husband with his settlement in the UK and with the family reunion application. She is a nice lady and she welcomed me with a lovely smile on her face, a bunch of flowers and some fruit. This was so important to me personally as I will not forget that moment and that nice smile on her wonderful face. She gave me the impression that we were welcome in her country, and at that moment I felt relieved and forgot about the whole lot of worries which were in my head. I had the feeling of safety, and I was excited to start a new life in the UK.

Acts of kindness

Rachael: Many people ask me, as a professional working with refugees, how they can help to welcome refugees and vulnerable migrants to their communities. This example here is perfect. Never underestimate the impact that a kind word, eye contact and a smile can have. Individuals new to the UK may have a lot of statutory and professional input (caseworkers, social workers, housing officers, GP liaisons etc), which is not a bad thing, but can make them feel somewhat faceless and like a small cog in a big system. Taking the time to make an individual feel known, seen and valued will never be a waste of time. Simple phrases such as *'It is so nice to meet you (and your family)'* or *'We're so glad you're here in the UK with us'* make it clear that they are entirely welcome. And these conversations stick with them, as you can read here!

A few days later, I realised that starting life in a new country, a different culture and a new system was not going to be as easy as I had expected after all. There were a lot of barriers to being integrated into a new culture and a new country. I was completely lost and confused. Fortunately, I got a lot of support from ICN (International Care Network), which is a charity that helps refugees and asylum seekers to rebuild their life here in the UK. As part of their remit, they are contracted by the local council to help support families in the area arriving on various resettlement schemes. At this time, they were working with Syrian families who were arriving on the Syrian Vulnerable Persons Resettlement Scheme (SVPRS). My family and I were not on that scheme, but they supported us as they help to support refugees in general. Not long after I arrived, they also asked me to work with them as an interpreter, which was a golden opportunity for me. Through this, I gained good experience because I used to go with my colleagues, the support workers from ICN, to interpret and support the new Syrian families coming to the UK.

I was so happy to help the Syrian refugees because I had the same experience. I know how they feel and the grand expectations that they may have had before their arrival. Most of the Syrians who are still in Syria or in other countries like Lebanon, Iraq and Jordan think that we are living in Paradise here in the UK and we have had no problems once we arrived here as it is a *'great foreign country'*. They do not know that we do, in fact, still have a lot of problems and concerns. They do not know how difficult it is to start a new life from the very beginning in a completely different culture. They may not realise how very hard it can be to live as a stranger and to live in a place where you may be misunderstood when you do something or say something that is interpreted differently than how you meant. They have not heard the horrible sentence *'if you are not happy here, why don't you go back to your country?'*. Yes, although I personally have not heard that sentence uttered to my face, I know others who have heard it. Some British people think that all refugees are poor homeless people who come from camps and tents looking to get money and live a better life depending on the benefits that they get from the government. They do not know that most of us used to have properties, good jobs, that we are educated but that we have lost everything suddenly and that we have fled our country looking for safety and to start a new life in a place where even our skills and qualifications are sometimes not recognised.

Reflective activity 1: 'Write your name backwards' activity

Without access to any further instructions, write your name backwards.

Did you write it from right to left? Did you write each letter backwards, or your name starting from the last letter to the first? It seemed like a simple instruction but was ambiguous. Imagine you're new to the country and someone has told you to register at the GP. Sounds simple enough, but how are you supposed to know where to start and which order tasks must be completed in? Different responses to how the instruction made you feel might include: confused, frustrated that a simple task was taking so long, feeling stupid that you had to ask for clarification, drained, enjoyed the challenge etc. There are many different responses to culture shock but it is important to note that *every* aspect of life takes up more mental energy than usual.

Reflective activity 2

If you have friends from different countries, ask them to talk about things like their name and where they're from in their mother-tongue language and then quiz you on their answers! Simple questions like these can even be frustrating and embarrassing when you know the answer but can't communicate that.

Settling here will be more complicated for those who arrive in the UK irregularly after an extremely hard and long journey. A person who has arrived in this way at a port of entry (eg airport) in the UK must make an application for asylum. This is a request to be recognised offically as a refugee. All asylum applications will be determined by the Home Office. Until an asylum application has been determined no action can be taken to require the departure of the asylum applicant or their dependents from the UK. If the Home Office decides to grant asylum, the Immigration Officer will grant one of various kinds of 'leave to remain'. If a person seeking leave to enter is refused asylum, the options are to appeal the decision, to take assisted repatriation or to undergo forced deportation. To apply for asylum, the Home Office will need to carry out various substantive interviews to examine the reasons asylum is being claimed for. There may also be a requirement to report to asylum centres or police stations at regular intervals. If the person fails to comply with the requirement to report to an Immigration Officer for examination, this can affect the outcome of their case. Applications can take anywhere from six months to over a year to receive a decision and there is very minimal communication in the meantime regarding the stage of the asylum application. This means a few months waiting with stress.

Difference between an asylum seeker and a refugee

The UK government accepts someone as a refugee if he or she has fled their own country because of a *'well-founded fear of being persecuted for reasons of race, religion, nationality, membership of a particular social group or political opinion'* (Geneva Convention on refugees, a United Nations agreement that the UK is signed up to). So, a refugee is a person who has been granted *leave to remain* in the UK for five years, and at the end of this period they can apply for *indefinite leave to remain*. An asylum seeker is a person who has *'left their country and is seeking protection from persecution and serious human rights violations in another country, but who hasn't yet been legally recognized as a refugee and is waiting to receive a decision on their asylum claim'* (Amnesty International, 2022a). One year after being granted indefinite leave to remain it is possible for a refugee to apply for British citizenship, at which point you have the right to hold a British passport. This whole process takes a minimum of six years and usually much longer.

The right to work (or not)

A key distinction between a refugee and an asylum seeker is that refugees have permission to work in the UK, and the rights to access public funds such as welfare benefits and health provision (NHS services). Most asylum applicants are not permitted to work while their applications are being considered. A Refugee Action Coalition report stated that *'People seeking asylum in the UK are only able to apply for the right to work after they have been waiting for a decision on their asylum claim for over a year. Even then, the few people who are granted such permission are rarely able to work in practice because their employment is restricted to the narrow list of highly skilled professions included on the Government's Shortage Occupation List'* (2018, p 3). There are figures about the negative cost this has on our economy.

Research conducted by the Lift the Ban Coalition (2020) (made up of over 200 organisations which have joined together to campaign for the right to work for people seeking asylum) indicates that the British government could benefit by up to £97.8 million per year if 50 per cent of those waiting more than six months for their asylum decision were working full time at the national average wage from their tax and National Insurance contributions and were no longer requiring subsistence support.

Not being permitted to work also negatively impacts language learning (most effectively carried out through immersion in an English-speaking environment) and an individual's self-confidence. The routine of employment, combined with the knowledge that you are contributing to the economy within which you are living, has an overwhelmingly positive effect on mental health as well as being of benefit to the wider community and economy.

In my case I had been granted refugee status even before my arrival as my husband had applied through the family reunion route. So, this was much easier for me and my children than my husband. This meant we could fly straight from Damascus, Syria to England when joining my husband, instead of having to go on that difficult journey. I have permission to work, and I have worked in the UK as an interpreter for several years, but recently I have had the feeling that I would really like to make the most of my experience and go back to teach in schools. However, it does feel like my ten years of teaching has been buried here in the UK. So, I compared my qualifications from Syria and I was so happy when I found out that my qualification was recognised here in the UK. I started to search for a job as a teaching assistant in primary schools, but I was shocked when I then realised that they require certain additional qualifications. Because I was determined to go back to teaching again, I did some courses online to train as a teaching assistant and then I contacted one of the schools just to get another shock when they said, '*You should have training in UK schools*'. I have also tried to fill in online applications. Again, they just say that I should put my teaching skills here in the UK and to mention two headteachers, based in the UK, as references. How can I get the skills if they do not accept my skills in Syria and yet they do not let me work with them to get the training?

When your identity and place in your community is stripped away – the concept of liminality

Transitioning to life in a new country, especially when fleeing conflict, can be disorientating. One way of considering this phenomenon is using the anthropological concept of liminality. Liminality is a concept developed by the anthropologist Victor Turner in the 1960s and 1970s. It describes the quality of ambiguity or disorientation that occurs in the middle stage of a rite of passage (when an individual leaves one group to join another), such as in the transition from child to adult or, in this case, when transitioning from one country, culture and community to another. Liminality refers to the middle stage when participants no longer hold their pre-ritual status but have not yet begun the transition to the status they will hold when the rite is complete (Turner, 1974). In their work with refugees, Overland et al (2014) explain that during a rite's liminal stage, participants '*stand at the threshold*' between their previous way of structuring their identity, time or community and a new way which completing the rite establishes.

More recently, usage of the term liminality has broadened to describe political and cultural change as well as rites of passage (Thomassen, 2009; Katznelson, 2021). In the introduction to his liminality and cultures of change paper, Horvath (2009) explains that during liminal periods of all kinds, social hierarchies may be reversed or temporarily dissolved, continuity of tradition may become uncertain, and future outcomes once taken for granted may be thrown into doubt.

If we consider an asylum seeker; we can see how the identities and community practices they used to use to structure their view of 'self' have been stripped away. They are no longer citizens of their home country; they are unable to work and identify as an employee or craftsperson/professional. Even their family links (and identities as 'son or daughter of') are removed in many ways. This dissolution of order during liminality creates a fluid, malleable situation that enables new institutions and customs to become established. This can, in some ways, be a positive experience, as people move beyond cultural and familial expectations placed on them and embrace new opportunities. However, we find that while asylum seekers are in this stage with no concrete indication of what the next step is (asylum claim accepted, asylum claim refused, appeal, voluntary or forced repatriation), this liminality more often has a negative effect on the individual's mental health because they have no solid ground on which to begin remolding or establishing their identity or plans for the future. Even for Ahed, who arrived with refugee status and has the right to work, doing so has presented many challenges with her extensive expertise and experience as a headteacher in Syria not being recognised in her search for employment as a teacher or teaching assistant in the UK.

You may ask now why I do not carry on with interpreting?

Interpreting was an excellent job for me because I learnt a lot about the community services offered locally and the welfare and health services available. I have gained a broad experience that has enabled me to help my family and others. As the system is completely different from our country, it was difficult to know how to settle in the UK. For example, when I arrived, I did not know how to register my children in schools, how to go to see a doctor or a dentist. In our country the healthcare system is different; you can choose the doctor, specialist or dentist that you would like without registering with the surgery and sometimes even without booking an appointment.

You can even go straight away for a free service at the hospital to see a specialist and when the specialist tells you that your symptoms or your health problems require you to see another specialist, they would advise you where to go and which clinic you can go to until you can see a suitable doctor. That is why Syrians often feel that they are neglected when they have to wait for an appointment to be booked, especially when they are put on the long-term list to get an appointment.

When I started my job as an interpreter with ICN, I learnt how to do a lot of things and I started to help others. At the beginning, I was so happy to help the Syrians because most of them have very little English and they struggle to do a lot of things because of their limited language. Although they would have support workers from ICN who helped them during the days of the week and even at the weekends in emergencies, they used to find it easier to contact me as I am from the same country and can speak the language they speak. However, the more I used to help them the more they would expect from me. Unfortunately, they were complaining a lot and this was difficult for me to hear. 'You are not doing your job properly', they said, although I used to help them a lot, even out of hours. Some of this is related to cultural expectations. The families would not always initially understand that we have to work within the system and that we cannot 'pull strings' to make things happen faster, such as speeding up the outcome of a benefits application or a referral to the hospital. They also did not necessarily grasp the boundaries placed on a professional interpreter. I was there simply to interpret what both parties were saying, but I was not a support worker, and this distinction was very difficult to manage.

This is what pushed me to stop interpreting and to start to think of my previous job as a teacher. On the one hand, I have faced a lot of difficulties and barriers here in the UK, such as trouble integrating with the community; challenges finding good jobs; missing my family, my relatives and my friends back in Syria; and missing our cultural celebrations, habits and practice of our religious rituals in our community. For example, during the month of Ramadan in Syria, the whole family gathers around the table for a meal at the same time. I would spend time with my sister and my mum preparing these meals. We have special prayers during Ramadan in the mosques, and you feel such a sense of community as everyone goes at the same time to the mosques to do these prayers. Even though it is a time commitment you feel that everyone is there; everyone is participating in something special that really refreshes your soul. Especially as it only happens once a year! Eid is the celebration at the end of Ramadan and during this time we normally visit all our relatives. You know you have time to do this and spend quality time with your loved ones because the time is set apart during this celebration, unlike when you are all working and busy. It feels that everyone is happy and during these days people help each other and give to the poor, so they can have new clothes and food. After one month of fasting, you feel you have really earnt this celebration! So, these times of celebrations in the UK do remind me of all I am missing while living here in England without my extended family. On the other hand, I live here with my children and husband in a safe place. I feel happy to see my children going to school every day and building their future and that they can find the daily basics, such as water, electricity, warmth and food, which is something most Syrians are struggling to find nowadays in Syria.

Although starting a new life in a new culture is difficult, this was an inevitable decision. When leaving our home country, we do not make this decision unless we believe we do not have another choice to keep our family safe. It is an introduction to starting a new life suddenly and the decision revolves around our children and the opportunities they face in life. As a mother, the safety of your children is the most important thing. Because I have sons, the reality is that when they are 17, they would be forced to join the military in Syria, which would put them in danger, and I wanted to avoid that happening. Now we are here, they have a much better future waiting for them. They can choose their own future instead of having decisions forced upon them and this is the biggest thing for me, to be honest.

A lot of the families I have met do not know how to talk about their stories, their traumas and the emotions that they struggle with. They may not have the words to explain these things, and they may be afraid of bringing up memories which are very painful. I can see that if you are able to talk about things that you are keeping inside, it can feel like such a relief. Sometimes stress can force you to act in ways you don't like or understand and finding ways to express this can really help. Culturally, it is less common for Syrians to talk about mental health and talking about these feelings causes feelings of shame. Therefore, it is common for families here to express physical symptoms when dealing with trauma, rather than being able to articulate their emotional and mental symptoms. They often present with symptoms such as stomach ache, chronic pain, headaches or nausea but no physical problem is found. Doctors here will explain that they believe the root of these problems is related to trauma or mental well-being, but this diagnosis is hard to understand for people who are hoping to be prescribed a medical treatment to deal with physiological symptoms.

Maslow's hierarchy of needs

In our experience at ICN, we find that the stress of waiting for a Home Office decision is the major barrier to accessing mental health support. In regard to the under-18 asylum seekers we support, it has been documented on several occasions that even when they take up the offer of support (cognitive behavioural therapy [CBT], counselling etc), their course of treatment is often terminated early by the professional in question, as it becomes clear that until they know whether they will be allowed to stay in the UK, they will be unable to address and resolve other trauma. Others acknowledge the fact that they are suffering from poor mental health but explain that until this decision has been finalised, they do not have the headspace to engage meaningfully with mental health or well-being interventions. However proactively they seek to improve their own well-being in the meantime, this one detail is a factor entirely out of their control, with such major implications that it tends to overcloud any other progress being made.

A useful way to understand this is by considering Maslow's hierarchy of needs. Maslow's hierarchy model was developed in the 1940s and is often depicted as a pyramid. Maslow suggested that basic needs will be prioritised over psychological and self-fulfilment needs and so these will need to be addressed first.

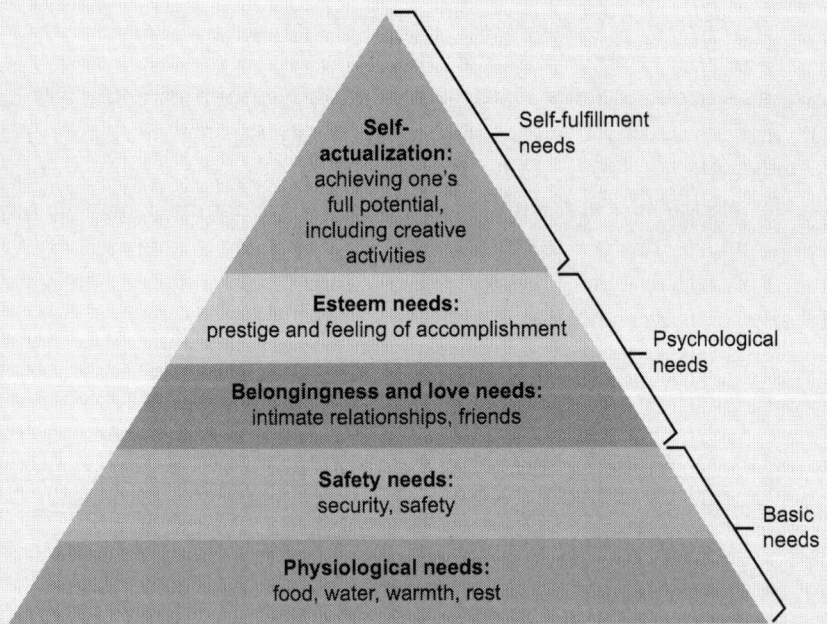

Figure 6.1 Maslow's hierarchy of needs
(McLeod, 2022)

The priority for asylum seekers and refugees will be on meeting their basic needs for food and shelter, safety and security, before they can start to address their psychological needs and the trauma they have experienced or be able to achieve a sense of belonging.

I am pleased I know people I can talk to about my story and my feelings, as I can see that it helps me to express these things. Just as I think it is a good relief for me to talk about what is going on inside of me, I would encourage other people who are in the same position to take out the bad memories. I envisage this as taking all these negative feelings and memories outside of their minds by speaking or by writing them down and then throwing them in the sea, or over a cliff for the wind to take them! It is very therapeutic to have a big cry or to write things down on a paper and then rip it up. This is hard to encourage, culturally, but hopefully the longer people stay in their new country the more willing they will be to give it a try, as they understand that it is not something shameful.

Suggested reading and viewing

» *Beekeeper of Aleppo* by Christy Lefteri.

» *Hope not Fear* by Hassan Akkad.

» *The Lightless Sky* by Gulwarli Passarlay.

» *A Thousand Splendid Suns/The Kite Runner* by Khaled Hosseini.

» *Ink Knows No Borders: Poems of the Immigrant and Refugee Experience* by Patrice Vecchione.

Suggested TV/film

» *For Sama* (Waad Al-Kateab).

» *Insyriated* (2017). Arabic audio, English subtitles.

» *Home* – Channel 4. A comedy series written by and starring Rufus Jones which deftly gets to the essence of home and family through Syrian asylum seeker Sami.

YouTube

» The official music video of Elton John's 'Rocket Man'. In his own interpretation of Elton John's iconic hit, Iranian filmmaker and refugee Majid Adin reimagines 'Rocket Man' to tell a new story of adventure, loneliness and hope.

» Syria TV is a channel which attempts to portray the situation in Syria as it is now. Viewer discretion advised as some videos may be distressing.

References

Amnesty International (2022a) Definitions: What Exactly Is a Refugee, Asylum Seeker and a Migrant? [online] Available at: www.amnesty.org/en/what-we-do/refugees-asylum-seekers-and-migrants/#:~:text=An%20asylum%2Dseeker%20is%20a,decision%20on%20their%20asylum%20claim (accessed 9 August 2022).

Amnesty International (2022b) Refugees, Asylum-seekers and Migrants. [online] Available at: www.amnesty.org/en/what-we-do/refugees-asylum-seekers-and-migrants (accessed 8 August 2022).

BBC Radio 4 (2016) The Syrian War. *PM.* [online] Available at: www.bbc.co.uk/programmes/p04dfsvp (accessed 8 August 2022).

Horvath, A (2009) Liminality and the Unreal Class of the Image-Making Craft: An Essay on Political Alchemy. *International Political Anthropology* 2(1): 53–72.

Katznelson, I (2021) Measuring Liberalism, Confronting Evil: A Retrospective. *Annual Review of Political Science*, 24(1): 1–19.

Lift The Ban Coalition (2020) *Lift The Ban: Why Giving People Seeking Asylum the Right to Work Is Common Sense.* [online] Available at: www.refugee-action.org.uk/wp-content/uploads/2020/07/Lift-The-Ban-Common-Sense.pdf (accessed 8 August 2022).

Macleod, H (2011) Syria: How It All Began. *The World*, 23 April. [online] Available at: https://theworld.org/stories/2011-04-23/syria-how-it-all-began (accessed 8 August 2022).

McLeod, S A (2022) Maslow's Hierarchy of Needs. *Simply Psychology.* [online] Available at: www.simplypsychology.org/maslow.html (accessed 8 August 2022).

Overland, G, Guribye, E and Lie, B (eds) (2014) *Nordic Work with Traumatised Refugees: Do We Really Care.* Newcastle: Cambridge Scholars Publishing.

ReliefWeb (2022) Informing Humanitarians Worldwide 24/7. [online] Available at: https://reliefweb.int (accessed 8 August 2022).

Statistica.com (2022) Number of Internally Displaced Persons in Syria 2012–2020. [online] Available at: www.statista.com/statistics/740245/number-of-internally-displaced-persons-in-syria/ (accessed 12 August 2022).

Thomassen, B (2009) The Uses and Meaning of Liminality. *International Political Anthropology*, 2(1): 5–28.

Turner, V (1974) Liminal to Liminoid, in Play, Flow, and Ritual: An Essay in Comparative Symbology. *Rice Institute Pamphlet – Rice University Studies*, 60(3). https://hdl.handle.net/1911/63159.

Refugee Action (2018) Lift the Ban: Why People Seeking Asylum Should Have the Right to Work. [online] Available at: www.refugee-action.org.uk/wp-content/uploads/2018/10/Lift-the-Ban-report.pdf (accessed 9 August 2022).

UNHCR (2021) *Mid-Year Trends 2021.* [online] Available at: www.unhcr.org/618ae4694.pdf (accessed 8 August 2022).

United Nations (1951) *Convention Relating to the Status of Refugees*, 28 July 1951, Geneva.

Chapter 7 | Being a parent in the child protection system

Christine Bondsfield and Tilia Lenz

When you see me now, you would not guess where I have come from…

I am 44 years old and a single mother of three boys: J is 23, L is 21 and E is 11 years old. We have been on a tough journey as a family and faced a lot of challenges on the way. Those challenges have meant that we were not always able to live together due to the way we were treated by professionals – we were excluded from being a family. I have jumped through so many bloody hoops to achieve where I am now, had to prove myself to people and professionals in particular. My friends and family knew who I was and always said that I put my kids first. I was shocked that people would see me in a different light. I was furious and frustrated that professionals were not listening to me and would not believe anything I said. I felt that whatever I was doing, it just wasn't good enough for any of them. I was labelled by my then husband and by professionals as: mentally unstable, drug and alcohol user, described as a bad mother and letting my children down. I wish for people to understand that my kids are my life, and I would do anything for them. I want to tell my story as a victim of domestic violence and abuse, how my family was torn apart as a result and how we healed together later.

Domestic abuse

There are some 2.3 million victims of domestic abuse a year aged 16 to 74 in the UK (two-thirds of whom are women) and more than one in ten of all offences recorded by the police are domestic abuse related. The Domestic Abuse Act 2021 created a statutory definition and is a new piece of legislation that emphasises that domestic abuse is not just physical violence, but can take the form of emotional and economic abuse and controlling and coercive behaviours. It places duties on local authorities in England to support victims, including children who are exposed to domestic abuse.

Source: Home Office (2021)

I have a physical disability caused by a neurological syndrome; this means I stumble, fall and bruise easily. So, when I got my first own place, a council flat at the age of 18, independence was a struggle. I had to leave my parents' house as there were six of us and it was very crowded with three girls in one room, and I was on the sofa bed sharing the space with my baby sisters.

My parents lived ten miles away and it was really difficult to get to them. Initially I had to take two buses across town for two hours each way, which was hard and tiring. All my friends lived on the other side of town as well and looking back, I felt sad, lonely and lost. Being so young and taking responsibility for my own home was tough: I had to buy my own food and manage bills, and this made me feel suffocated at times. I had to be a 'grown up' when my friends were still able to enjoy parties, shopping and 'girly things', while I got my driving test done to be able to get on the road.

I met D at a party and he shortly afterwards moved in with me – he probably saw my vulnerabilities straight away and coming to stay with me was an easy option for him; he literally had a made bed waiting. Initially I felt special and loved by him but didn't realise then that the abuse in our relationship was there from the beginning. He would tell me that I looked silly in heels and that I could not dance like the other girls due to my disability. That really hurt, and I would be upset but then he would make it up to me and be kind and gentle. Now I can see that this is very much the cycle of abuse, though not then – it was mind games from the start.

Coercive control

Coercive control is when the perpetrator of abuse seeks to take away the victim's sense of self, minimises their freedom to do things and is violating their human rights. The Serious Crime Act 2015 created a new offence of controlling or coercive behaviour. It is still a challenge for victims, society and professionals alike to recognise this kind of abuse as it often is an 'undercurrent' of a relationship. By reflecting on how it would feel for you to be told that you are *never enough but always too much*, you can develop an understanding for the challenges of victims. This kind of abuse gets to the core of your personality, without leaving any visible marks.

Further reading: Research in Practice for Adults (2016)

Looking back, if people would have listened then, if they'd have taken care to see what was going on, then I would not have gone through all the trauma, despair and anguish.

D would often disappear for days and tell his friends that we were never together. He would then come home and I was not allowed to tell people that we were a couple. He would go out with my girly friends and would unashamedly flirt with them – he even snogged a girl in a club in front of me while I was heavily pregnant! He tried to get to me and tried to get a reaction. On the other hand, he would be so jealous if I would even just talk to a man. He would start fights in a pub over this and now I know alarm bells should have been ringing. He was mean and said horrible things to me before we went on a night out, so I would be deeply upset and feel terrible about myself. The next day, he would just be lovely. It really screwed with my head and I felt confused. I could not work out why he acted in this way; there was never any explanation – I always thought it was my fault.

Over the 18 years of our relationship, D was physically, mentally, financially, emotionally and sexually abusive towards me; on reflection, he probably was really jealous of the relationship I had with our children. He played cruel mind games and told me that I was bipolar and I was a useless mum, and I think at some point I just behaved in that way – as I believed him. It became a self-fulfilling prophecy.

Deciding to leave

Do you wonder why victims of abuse don't just leave? Women's Aid share that there is a huge rise in the likelihood of violence after separation. Women are exposed to the blame from the perpetrator, society and professionals, just like Christine experienced. People often focus on why the victim stayed rather than on why the perpetrator continues to abuse. Living in constant fear and terror impacts on your self-esteem and victims have limited freedom to make decisions about their own lives.

Source, support and further reading: Women's Aid (2022)

At 16, I came out of school with no GCSEs and with a diagnosis of dyslexia; school was quite tough. My parents were not academically minded, and I came from a proper working-class family where my mum and dad gave us a roof over the head and clothes. But there was little emotional warmth, cuddles and hugs.

There was never any encouragement to achieve or want more in life. But I wanted more; I wanted to experience other things and do stuff. Looking back, I have a lot of fire and passion inside me, and I always wanted to help others.

When D put me down and controlled me so much, I was disappointed and angry with myself for feeling so useless. Though instead of keeping my head down, I could not hide my ambitions anymore. So, at 23 years old I set off and gained qualifications in youth and community work while I was a looking after my two oldest boys and D.

I worked for the youth services for years and then for housing providers, supporting high-risk individuals. From there I got involved with offenders, ex-offenders and probation services, visited prisons and worked with people to 'stay on track'. When I was 29, I started to support young mums-to-be through parenting classes, working in in partnership with the local authorities. My confidence in my achievements grew and I felt I was at last becoming myself and reaching my potential! I earned a good income and was respected as a professional. I attended meetings around child protection and knew the system. I was established in my work and in hindsight probably played my professional role really well in order to cope with what was going on at home.

D was very jealous of this and didn't like that I was successful and essentially had my own life. He accused me of having affairs with colleagues. D jeopardised a lot of my work; one day he threw out my training portfolio and he deleted whole essays from my laptop. He told me that no one liked me at work and my efforts on the job were never valued. Although my work was really emotionally tough and draining, I was never allowed to be tired, yet I was mentally exhausted from work and my home life. D never helped with the kids, didn't do anything in the household and I felt like a single mum with a grumpy adult child who threw tantrums if he didn't get his way.

But instead of splitting up from him, I thought I needed stability and a secure base in my life. Looking back, it feels surreal that I asked D to make a commitment to us. Yet we got married and continued our lives together and I fell pregnant with E in 2010.

D was very controlling. He budgeted everything and I was only allowed to wear certain brands, go shopping in specific shops and only able to buy high-end foods and clothes. We clearly lived above our limits and it was not until much later that I realised that D had got us into significant debt and not paid the mortgage for our house.

Over the years, D's controlling behaviours became just normal to me and, reflecting on it, I just did as I was told – even when D made me take drugs and use alcohol. When he wanted to have sex, he gave me cocaine so I would be 'up for it'. He controlled me so much, I did not know how to say no – this was all I ever knew.

In November 2011, things really escalated. D had been out on the drink one night and I was in bed. When he came home, he wanted sex and I was not up for it; it was 1am and I was really tired from looking after baby E and working all day. He got so angry and very violently sexually assaulted me; he got hold of me and smacked my head against the wall, threw me onto the bed and strangled me.

I had a black eye and was in a lot of pain, so reported it to the police the day after it happened. I told D that he was a monster and he handed himself into the police. This weirdly resulted in the assault being dealt with in a way as if it was not a crime – they had their perpetrator and only needed a statement from me. When they came to talk to me, there was no empathy from the police officer. I had no support as a victim; no photos were taken – the interview was conducted by a male officer, in my home with my baby on my lap. I felt sick that the whole thing was minimised and the effect that the sexual assault had on my body was not even considered or acknowledged. The professional response reiterated that I was worthless, while I was hurting inside and my emotions were in turmoil. I did not feel listened to; I even felt blamed for what happened. What an absolute joke; these people were meant to protect me, and I felt so let down by the police.

D was out on bail with conditions not to contact me, but he still did. He told me that he missed the boys and the boys wanted to see him. They did not understand what was going on.

Then D promised me to change; he apologised. D asked his female friend to 'help' me write a witness statement, saying that this incident was not that serious and that it was just a normal 'domestic'. She typed it for me to hand to the courts. He was convicted and got put onto the Sex Offenders Register for seven years. He had to attend a course for domestic violence and abuse perpetrators to change his behaviour. Looking back, he was in full control of the situation, and the systems and professionals that should have supported me and the children as victims did not kick in and were blinded by D's narrative.

Number of domestic abuse related incidents

The Office for National Statistics states that the number of domestic abuse related incidents recorded by the police in England and Wales increased by 6 per cent in the year 2020 to 2021. This ended a trend of consecutive annual decreases seen in recent years. Calls to the National Domestic Abuse Helpline, run by the charity Refuge, saw an increase of 22 per cent in that period. There was a sharp increase of calls during the lockdown periods. The Crown Prosecution Service state that in the first quarter of 2020, domestic abuse accounted for 52 per cent of their caseload.

Source: ONS (2021) and CPS (2022)

Following this violation, we had the perfect year! D was on his best behaviour; I could not have felt more loved, worshipped and I at last had the marriage I always wanted, being on cloud nine. But the minute the court orders and probation supervision stopped, he returned to his old self with a vengeance.

In June 2013 our marriage hit crisis point – we were both on drugs and I was taking cocaine as a coping mechanism to just get through the day. I only weighed six stone; I was a shadow of myself and felt empty. No one really knew what was going on, while I was in a living hell of abuse, coercion and violence.

We decided that we would have a break and he moved out to a so-called friend's flat. It turned out that they then started an affair and he manipulated her to abuse me through mind games.

One night he gave me a mix of drugs and when I was at my lowest told me that the crux of our marital issues was E. He tried to convince me that it would all be good if E was dead – I should kill him! I was distraught and off my head; in my mind I knew that this was not right but the years of manipulation had manifested themselves. I always had to do what D told me to do and when he said that E was evil, I was so scared that I started to self-harm and deeply cut my arms.

Somehow, I was able to call a friend who got me out of the house and sought help. I was so scared and confused. I subsequently had a mental breakdown and was voluntarily admitted to a psychiatric hospital.

Mental health treatment and support

The charity Mind explains that:

Most people with mental health problems are able to get treatment and support at home, sometimes with the help of their GP. But there may be times when you need to go to hospital to get treatment. You are a voluntary patient (sometimes called an informal patient) if you are having in-patient treatment in a psychiatric hospital of your own free will. You should have capacity to understand that you are going into hospital and agree to treatment for your mental health problem.

Source and support: Mind (2018)

D came to the hospital and told me that I should not be there but should be at home and look after the boys. Staff saw all of this and sent D away. They kept me safe at a time when I was most vulnerable and I felt understood and listened to for the first time by professionals.

It was then when children's social care (CSC) became involved and undertook assessments for my children.

As I was in hospital, I could not look after my boys and they were taken into care under section 20 of the Children Act 1989.

A social worker from local authority A came to ask me to sign a piece of paper without properly explaining what it was. I was still not well and didn't quite understand what this really meant until I tried to get my children back in my care and I was told no! Professionals had formed a view of me and put labels of 'mental', unfit mother and drug user on me – a lot of it was the narrative from D, who was still controlling the situation. The added challenge was that my marital home was in local authority A and I was told by the social workers not to go back there as D could get to me and the children, so I sought housing in the neighbouring local authority B. The older boys had gone to stay with their paternal grandparents in local authority A and were dealt with by CSC there. E had come with me to live in local authority B – he had not been accommodated and the assessments from CSC in local authority B were positive towards me and they subsequently closed the case. I felt that I had a good working relationship with the social worker from local authority B and they listened to what had happened to me and the boys. But local authority A continued to go with D's version of me being *'mental and a bad mother'.*

Taking a child into care

The concept of 'voluntary accommodation' for children to be taken into care by the local authority is set out in section 20 of the Children Act 1989. This has been misused by local authorities in the past who asked parents to give consent to remove children from their care or else the police or court would remove them (so is it really voluntary?). In 2015, the judge Sir James Munby, then President of the Family Division, urged for changes in practice. There have been significant challenges in family courts around this as parents previously had been prevented from having the children back in their care. Section 20 arrangements are made without legal representation for the parents or the child and cause an ethical dilemma for social work practice if no informed consent can be sought, like in Christine's case.

While all of this was happening, my family, my children and my home were taken from me through D's actions; I also lost my job. I was told that I could not undertake the work with vulnerable people anymore as I was 'in the system' myself now. I felt that I had lost everything I had ever wanted, everything that I ever worked for. Just imagine losing your home, your kids, your marriage and your job all at once! Looking back, I don't know how I was able to keep going. I had no anchor, no point of reference in my life and trying to get back on my feet was incredibly difficult. Professionals and D continued to label me while I tried to convince them that I really just wanted to do the best for my kids.

I tried to make a living for E and myself and to get on as a small family unit. However, in June 2014, D and his then partner broke into my home and beat me up – I was so scared! E was in the house and I was so worried that he would wake up. I was covered in bruises and with the prolonged stress and trauma D had inflicted on me, I did not know how to go on. I tried to overdose while E was in the home with me – I did not know any other way out. But somehow I did not die, yet I was so low I could not go on either. The mental health worker who assessed me at the time was scared that I would die if she did not get me help.

At this point local authority B opened the case for E again and were very worried about his safety with me. They asked me to sign section 20 for him and placed him with my sister. The social worker shared what this meant and explained the legal context and that I could make an informed decision.

I was still so controlled by D that I struggled to engage with professionals and tell them the truth of my experiences. However, they just saw me as aggressive and non-compliant, not acknowledging the trauma I had been through. I just wished for people to understand that I was essentially a trapped animal in a cage and I felt threatened and scared.

When I tried to get all my children back, local authority A took the case to court and after long discussions with the judge, it was agreed that they would take the proceedings for all children forward. The professionals again had formed the view that I was an 'unfit mother' and were considering adoption as a plan for E – he was only a toddler! It would not just be me losing my son but my boys would lose their brother. The judge could see my struggles but said that I needed more time to sort myself out than E had; he needed to have a safe and stable home and at the time I was not able to give this to him – I was still struggling with health, perceived mental ill health, drink and drugs.

All this time D had unlimited contact with the boys and it really hurt to see that he was able to have such a different relationship with them than I could have. He had managed to twist the story to professionals and was seen as the wonderful dad and husband and I was the wicked one.

The court process was tough on me; I tried to show that I could be a good mum to the boys and undertook all the assessments but it wasn't enough to convince the professionals that I could care for the boys. The judge made the decision that the older boys should stay with their grandparents and E with my sister under a special guardianship order. I was told that I would need to make significant changes in my life, and this would take time. Although I had the 'all clear' for mental health after a psychiatric assessment and drug test through hair strand tests, I was still giving inconsistent results in my blood tests. This resulted in me being labelled as having an alcohol dependency.

I was totally confused and angry about this, thinking that there was a conspiracy against me as I was not drinking and I had done all the courses and assessments they had asked me to do. I jumped through all the hoops and yet I wasn't good enough! I was scared to lose my son but also scared to lose myself. My life was a constant battle and everyone was watching me. I could not fail and was on tenterhooks, feeling controlled not just by D but by the system and professionals around me.

One and a half years later, I had made it – I got a place for myself and was not drinking or taking drugs. I was ready to fight for my children and went back to court. I could also prove that I had never been an alcoholic but due to my underlying health condition, my liver was affected, explaining the inconsistency in the blood tests.

I was seen by the same judge as before and represented myself. He was really happy to see my progress and heard the case, coming to the conclusion that I could have E back! He applauded me to have made big changes in my life and being stable with my overall health. Local authority B was given a supervision order for three months, just in case we needed support.

In 2020, I eventually got the support I needed. I had suffered night terrors for years and felt that I needed to finally face my fears. Through the school I got a parent support adviser. It was really hard to ask for help, as it is always in the back of my head that I would get judged straight away. My history of mental ill health, overdose and domestic abuse will always stay with me, and I will always be labelled and seen as such by professionals. So, to approach the school for support was tough but worth it! Stepping out of my 'normal' patterns of behaviour was challenging but putting my experiences into perspective and seeing things for what they were was the way forward. I can now analyse situations without thinking that drink and drugs are the only coping mechanisms in life. I feel incredibly proud of myself to have managed this, considering this was at the height of the Covid-19 pandemic when the whole world was upside down.

Reflective activity

Falling back into old patterns of behaviours or 'relapse' is very common and part of recovery. We can have 'toxic' relationships with people; (mis)use food, medication, drugs or alcohol; and develop certain ways of thinking about ourselves and others. Leaving those patterns behind and changing our ways of managing emotional and physical pain is really hard. Government statistics show that of the people in drug and alcohol treatment in 2020, 47 per cent completed this free from dependence.

Source and support: Centrepoint (2018)

Take some time to reflect on the complex situation and the layers of patterns and relationships that Christine had to face and how they are interlinked. What added to her situation?

I eventually got to undertake therapy to help me look at the sexual assault. We worked on the trauma that I had experienced, which resulted in the anger I expressed towards professionals. I realise now how many failings were made in my case and I can see why so few women come forward to report domestic violence and abuse. Professionals need to understand the cycle of abuse and how this impacts on families without labelling the victims as '*not acting protectively*' and not prioritising the child's needs. Some social workers only saw me as an angry manic woman, while others cared to listen and saw beyond my fear-fuelled communication (telling them to fuck off and banging my hand on the table. Then I told the social worker to put a fucking rocket up her arse because she didn't do anything).

Fast forward to 2022, I am working for a local charity, working with families who need support. No one knows that I was 'in the system' for a long time. My manager is aware of my past but the professionals I am working with don't know my story – this means they don't judge me but see me as the hard-working woman that I am. I 'know my stuff' and am an advocate for vulnerable people in my day-to-day job. I have been able to fall back onto my qualifications and can see that domestic abuse can impact on anyone with huge consequences.

I have done a lot of work on myself, gone to domestic abuse courses for victims and can see how D manipulated me from such a young age. I have done the Pattern Changing course twice and, on reflection, the first time round I probably wasn't in the right frame of mind – at times there was such a strong pull towards D and I felt I still needed him. It takes time to rebuild the trust in oneself – the ability to stand on your own feet and be your own person. I can now see that dealing with 'freedom' after years of being trapped was a real challenge and at times overwhelming while fighting to have my family back.

Cycle **of grief**

On the one hand, Christine went through the 'Cycle of grief' with its stages of denial, anger, bargaining, depression and acceptance, while on the other hand she was stepping out of the cycle of abuse. Centre Point raise awareness of the fact that 16–24 year-olds have the highest rates of domestic abuse from a partner. Christine had to unlearn her 'truth' that she did not have rights and find courage to speak up for herself and her children.

Source and support: Centrepoint (2018)

I have spent most of my adult life in a situation where I was put down, controlled and hurt, while having to justify to professionals that I can be a good mum and do my job! I know that I didn't do everything right or in the best interest of my children; I can see that now. But the label I was given I feel sometimes sticks and I am still working hard to move on. The relationship between me and D is now amicable and he sees E regularly but in all of our communication I am mindful of how far I have come. I will not be put down anymore and I am proud of how much I have grown as a person. So now I am in a position to challenge social exclusion and can share my story to challenge the perception of others.

For professionals I wish that they would take the time to listen to the people they work with and look beyond the behaviours that the service users may present. Using less professional jargon and speaking to people properly and not talking down to them is what's needed to build relationships. The constant changes in social workers really impacted on us.

Women die because they go through experiences like I did without support – I was lucky because I had the support of my family and friends who were there for me when I was at my lowest. Others don't have that and if they don't get killed by their abusive partners, they get so run down by the system that they give up, give up their children for adoption or fostering, or the only way out appears to be suicide. When you feel worthless, discredited and lost, it feels that it is all happening in a daydream. For me, professionals reiterated that sense until I found my inner strength and started fighting. Now I feel a lot stronger, understanding the cycle of abuse and won't be manipulated or intimidated by D or anyone else. I am not scared anymore; look how far I have come!

References

Centrepoint (2018) Breaking the Cycle of Abuse. [online] Available at: https://centrepoint.org.uk/about-us/blog/breaking-the-cycle-of-abuse (accessed 8 August 2022).

Children Act 1989 [online] Available at: www.legislation.gov.uk/ukpga/1989/41/contents (accessed 8 August 2022).

Crown Prosecution Service (2022) Domestic Abuse. [online] Available at: www.cps.gov.uk/crime-info/domestic-abuse (accessed 8 August 2022).

Domestic Abuse Act 2021 [online] Available at: www.legislation.gov.uk/ukpga/2021/17/contents/enacted (accessed 8 August 2022).

Home Office (2021) Domestic Abuse Act 2021: Overarching Factsheet. [online] Available at: www.gov.uk/government/publications/domestic-abuse-bill-2020-factsheets/domestic-abuse-bill-2020-overarching-factsheet (accessed 8 August 2022).

Mind (2018) Voluntary Patients. [online] Available at: www.mind.org.uk/information-support/legal-rights/voluntary-patients/about-voluntary-patients (accessed 8 August 2022).

Office for National Statistics (ONS) (2021) Domestic Abuse in England and Wales Overview: November 2021. [online] Available at: www.ons.gov.uk/peoplepopulationandcommunity/crimeandjustice/bulletins/domesticabuseinenglandandwalesoverview/november2021 (accessed 8 August 2022).

Public Health England (2020) *Adult Substance Misuse Treatment Statistics 2019 to 2020: Report.* [online] Available at: www.gov.uk/government/statistics/substance-misuse-treatment-for-adults-statistics-2019-to-2020/adult-substance-misuse-treatment-statistics-2019-to-2020-report (accessed 8 August 2022).

Research in Practice for Adults (2016) Coercive Control. [online] Available at: https://coercivecontrol.ripfa.org.uk (accessed 8 August 2022).

Serious Crime Act 2015 [online] Available at: www.legislation.gov.uk/ukpga/2015/9/contents/enacted (accessed 8 August 2022).

Women's Aid (2022) Home Page. [online] Available at: www.womensaid.org.uk (accessed 8 August 2022).

Chapter 8

Being HIV positive

Samantha Dawson and Mel Hughes

Never in my life did I think that I would belong to a group of people who would experience social exclusion.

My name is Samantha, and I am 55 years old. I have two children and two grandchildren (biological), then I have an extended family daughter. She has three children, taking my grandchildren count up to five. I lived in a small village until I was 12 so I think it was even more protected living in such a small place. I have memories of playing at the rubbish dump and fishing down the river and going to the pictures with my best mate and his big brothers to watch James Bond movies. My nan and grandad on my maternal side were a massive part of my growing up and life felt simpler.

We moved to the seaside town I live now when I was 12 and then things changed quite a lot. Teenage things happened, I left home when I was 16 and then lived quite a difficult life.

Most people my age and above remember the tombstone advert about HIV and AIDS in the 1980s and talk about what it meant to them. To be honest I do not really remember it from my childhood, nor do I remember being told about HIV or even discussing the *'Don't Die of Ignorance'* message. I am not looking to blame anybody for the lack of information on this subject, but I often wonder why. I think (and this is only my opinion) that despite the message being meant for everybody, the media highlighted the groups that were being wiped out from this virus and this made people that were not in these groups feel safe and that it was not going to affect them.

Don't Die of Ignorance campaign

In 1986 and 1987, a government-led public health awareness campaign titled *'AIDS: Don't Die of Ignorance'* was shown on televisions around the nation. The shock tactics of the adverts were to ensure that people read a leaflet that was posted out to every home. The message warned the nation about a new virus that affected men and women. However, while the message may have been useful for an advertisement slogan, by focusing on death, the narrative created was one of doom and at the same time stigmatised the people already affected.

Reflective activity

https://youtu.be/iroty5zwOVw

https://youtu.be/sTBOHKAs0Eg

Take a moment to watch the adverts. Put yourself in the shoes of people watching it at the time. How does it make you feel? How might it have been experienced by people who already had a diagnosis of HIV or AIDS or were close to people who were affected?

Fast forward to 19 March 2008 when I was 40: I was at a routine visit to a sexual health clinic with a friend due to sex with an ex ending in me suspecting that I had a sexually transmitted infection (STI). I had got tested the week previous and been called back. The sun was shining, and my news was delivered. I was being told that I was now HIV positive. Wow, I was super shocked and just thought I was going to die.

I would like to say that I do not remember that day with so much detail, but I do. For March it was an unusually sunny day, and it was like my friend and me were on a day out. We drove to the hospital not knowing what was ahead. I was called into a room, a very typical hospital square room with lots of posters and leaflets about sexual health and there was the health adviser. I sat down, still no idea what was about to be said, but then she spoke. I cannot hear the first part, but I can hear the part when she says: *'Your HIV test has come out as positive.'* I had had it longer than six months but no longer than five years.

When I had first turned up for my sexual health screening, I will be honest and say I had not been that many times in my lifetime. It felt shameful. People do not want to make eye contact. There was a separate waiting room for women, away from the main reception area. You're given a number, no names, like it gave you some sort of invisibility cloak, only it didn't. People could still see you; they just didn't know your name. My number was called, and we discussed why I was there and what tests I would be having. I was offered an HIV test. We discussed it in some detail, and it was deemed that I would be low risk for HIV, but I thought that since I had grown up through the 80s and 90s and the AIDS epidemic it would not hurt to have the test. A blood test was taken but to be honest that was the last thing that I thought would come back as positive.

I do not remember what I said, but the shock on my face was the giveaway. *'Shall I get your friend?'* I heard her say. I was numb and just said yes. My friend came into the room, and I told her the news. She started to wail and scream like it had just happened to her and it continued like that for the rest of the appointment. The health adviser was lovely and told me what was going to happen next, then gave me some more appointments and lots of leaflets. I left the room, and the sun was still shining. The phone rang, and my friend answered it and wailed loudly, *'She's HIV positive'* and cried some more.

I went home and put all the leaflets under my mattress, only looking at them when I thought it was safe and no one was going to come into my room. I just hoped nobody could see it. One thing I thought that would help with the disguise was hats and sunglasses. This quickly became my signature look. I did not want anybody to look at me just in case they could see. I felt so dirty and did not like looking at myself and felt like I had no control. This lack of control led me to developing an eating disorder where I did not eat for days. Being in control of my calorie intake led me to losing a lot of weight and not once did I associate that with my HIV. My vision of being thin made me think that I looked healthy and that, combined with my signature look, no one would find out or need to know how disgusting I was or felt.

Prevalence of HIV in England

According to government figures, in 2020 there were approximately 97,740 people living with HIV in England. It is thought that approximately 4660 people are unaware that they are living with HIV, highlighting the importance of HIV testing (UK Health Security Agency, 2021).

Although the number of new diagnoses of HIV continues to fall and has done since 2005, diagnosis rates vary between different groups. The Terrence Higgins Trust (2022) reports that in 2019 there was a 10 per cent drop in new diagnoses from 2018 and a 34 per cent drop compared to 2014. The drop was even greater among gay and bisexual men (18 per cent). Diagnoses in women however only declined by 4 per cent. Women account for 28 per cent of new diagnoses. Over half of people receiving HIV specialist care in the UK in 2019 were white (53,621 – 54.6 per cent), and just over a quarter were Black African (28,525 – 28.7 per cent).

You can read more about the current figures and reasons for them from the following sources:

www.nat.org.uk/about-hiv/hiv-statistics

https://assets.publishing.service.gov.uk/government/uploads/system/uploads/attachment_data/file/1037215/hiv-2021-report.pdf

www.hiv.gov/hiv-basics/overview/history/hiv-and-aids-timeline

When I look back at this day, it is now an HIV anniversary, a celebration mixed up with many emotions. If I had been diagnosed in the early days of the epidemic, a celebration would have been a luxury that many did not get to experience. So yes, it may seem strange but it's more than just a celebration. It reminds me of how I felt on that day, all things I have learnt since and how far I have come.

I must admit, it did at first seem embarrassing going to the sexual health clinic. Now however it is just routine. Some tests are swabs and the room is very clinical, the usual hospital sink etc, a bed with stirrups so that your legs are up in the air while the nurse asks you to move your bum down to the edge of the bed and then they start discussing what kind of day you have been having. HIV and syphilis are blood tests. The room that the blood was taken from was reasonably small and unbeknown to me at that time would become my regular chair and room.

The clinic is in a new setting now, but when I tested positive it was based in the hospital in the same corridor as maxillofacial/dentistry. It was separated into two parts: men in the main reception part and women tucked to the side. The health adviser's room was full of posters and leaflets and little purple bags full of condoms and lubes. The health adviser was lovely and became a massive part of my journey although at that time I didn't know that was going to happen. Seeing all the posters made me realise some of the things I knew hardly anything about. How had I got to the age of 40 with such little knowledge of something that is so important? Sexual health is a part of your overall health and should be regarded as such and there should be no shame in it either. After being diagnosed, I used to think I wish was I going to the dentist department instead of the GUM clinic every time I walked down that corridor. It seemed not such a shameful department; however, after nearly 14 years of walking down that corridor the shame diminished, and I used to think how funny it was that I felt so bad; it became routine and just part of my life.

Sexual health

Sexual health or GUM clinics (genitourinary medicine) provide services covering sexual health. This can include sexually transmitted infection (STI) testing and family planning (contraception and pregnancy). All services are completely free and confidential. Information will not be shared, not even with your GP. Services are available to everyone from the age of 13 years upwards.

The NICE Impact Sexual Health report (2019) considers how NICE's evidence-based guidance contributes to improvements in sexual health.

Reflective activity

How do you feel about accessing a sexual health or GUM clinic to get tested?

At first being HIV + felt very dirty and I self-stigmatised myself so many times, but that was the fear of dying and the fear of not knowing how I was going to tell my family, my children and friends. The feeling of being dirty runs deep at the beginning and for some this may never change. I remember removing all the stuff from the bathroom which I thought needed to be removed in case I infected my family. Even though I knew this was not true, I did not want people to use my cup or share my drinks. The sight of blood was too much to cope with, and my bodily fluids felt dangerous. I felt like I was a risk to society. Feeling like a risk to society weighed so heavy on my mind, it grew into anxiety. Generalised anxiety stole my identity even further. It is like a part of me had died already. How was I going to work? How I was going to live? Would I ever fall in love again? Would I ever find anybody that wanted to be with somebody like me, some-body that is a danger? I lost the ability to function, to be me, not that I knew who that was anymore. I was living with a secret. My mum and dad knew but I had not told my children, who then still lived at home. I used to Google symptoms that could be seen as similar so that I could explain my huge weight loss and my sudden desire not to leave the house. For hours I would scan the symptoms of lupus. At least this didn't make me dirty or a risk to others. At least people would not think bad of me, my children would not need to feel ashamed, and it would not look like I had let my parents down.

Reducing **HIV transmission**

A UNAIDS (2022) worldwide target was to achieve 90–90–90 as part of a larger campaign to end all HIV transmission by 2030. This means that of the 106,980 people living with HIV in the UK, 90 per cent of all of these people should know their HIV status, 90 per cent of these same people should be on ART (anti-retroviral therapy) and 90 per cent of these people should be virally suppressed (meaning that their HIV is undetectable and they cannot pass it on). We have reached beyond those targets in the UK by achieving 95 per cent of people living with HIV knowing their status. 99 per cent are on HIV treatment and 97 per cent of these people are virally suppressed (HIV i-Base 2021).

The advancement in HIV medication and the changes in guidelines which focus on 'treatment as prevention' have meant that these targets have been met. With good adherence, a person living with HIV starting medica-tion within six months of diagnosis will become virally suppressed. This is more widely known as an undetectable viral load. U (undetectable) equals U (untransmittable); a fantastic place to be as somebody living with HIV.

> It means that HIV cannot be passed on to others, including sexual partners even with condomless sex.
>
> **Activity**
>
> To read more about the success of early diagnosis and HIV treatment, read:
>
> https://i-base.info/u-equals-u

For me, becoming undetectable made me feel that I was no longer a risk to society due to the previous stigma and self-stigma that I had experienced. Medication has also been simplified and despite the regime of an everyday tablet at the same time of day every day, having tablets that are less toxic and can be as simple as one tablet a day is something that is the difference between good and bad quality of life.

The clinic that I attended had referred me to a support centre for people living with HIV and this was a turning point in my rollercoaster ride. This is where I met others who taught me not to self-stigmatise. I am a human being, not perfect. This is a process that does not happen overnight. For me it took nearly three years before I started to see beyond my diagnosis. Due to the guidelines at the time, I did not start medication for nearly five years. I was ill every year and even hospitalised on quite a few occasions. When I eventually did start treatment, it was like being diagnosed all over again. This may seem a strange thing to say, but every day was a challenge then; all of a sudden, I had to factor in a tablet regime that was time sensitive. The first medication I started on needed a calorific quantity to be taken with it. This was difficult for somebody with an eating disorder. I struggled on this medication for a while and then was put on something different. Each time there were different side effects to deal with and I will be honest and say that I did not know I was even experiencing them; I thought that it was just part of having HIV. So, I suffered in silence and just got on with taking it every day. Every day, I had to set an alarm to encourage me to take it and it used to make me sad just the thought of it. It perpetuated the feeling of being dirty. It made it feel real.

My lack of sexual health knowledge and subconscious discrimination about HIV made it so hard some days. I did not want to look at myself and felt like I had no control over my future. Suddenly, I was no longer Sam; I was HIV Sam. It defined who I was, it controlled my doomed future, it made people feel sorry for me, it made my parents worry all the time, it was a great big curtain of gloom.

I had so many questions. How would I ever do anything again? How would I work? How would I have sex? How would I still be a parent? Just HOW?!!!!!!

Who was to blame for all this mess: my ex-boyfriend (who my friend had automatically assumed had given it to me) or me for not taking better care of myself, for not knowing more? It turns out it was not my ex that I had acquired HIV from. It was hard to think that I may never know. I have my suspicions and I am just so lucky that in the possibly five years I had been living with HIV before diagnosis, I had not passed it on to anybody else, something that I would never want to do.

Now my diagnosis means something completely different. I am living with HIV, and it does not define who I am as a human being, but it does mean that I experience social exclusion.

HIV and social exclusion

By being socially excluded, people living with HIV face further problems like barriers to accessing services and employment. Exclusion equals discrimination and the Equality Act 2010 gives people living with HIV protection and makes the discrimination unlawful. In employment for example there is no legal obligation to tell an employer your HIV status unless you are in a front-line armed forces position or performing invasive procedures, eg as a surgeon.

The advantages of being able to tell an employer would be the ability to have time off for appointments, reasonable adjustments in the workplace and flexible working hours. Many people living with HIV fear telling employers about their HIV status due to the fear of repercussions in the workplace or not even being offered employment. Discrimination in the workplace seems to be based on common myths and misconceptions that are often linked to either outdated knowledge and/or limited knowledge. Ignorance and misinformation does not make the discrimination right, but it may be why employers or work colleagues may unknowingly be discriminative.

In April 2000, a supermarket manager after being diagnosed with HIV was advised by the company to leave and go on gardening leave. They stated that staff did not want to work with him and having him as an employee would mean the company's profits would suffer.

This is an example of why maybe employment rates for people living with HIV are often found to be under the national average (National AIDS Trust,

2012). To improve workplace stigma and discrimination, the Positive Allies foundation was launched by the University of Sunderland. Employees displaying the Positive Allies Charter Mark are showing people living with HIV that there is no exclusion in their workplace.

Reflective activity

Are there employers that you can share the Positive Allies Charter Mark with?

When I think about how other people see me or other people living with HIV, I like to think that they do not see anything different. We certainly do not look any different, but it's just the look in people's eyes when you tell them something as simple as you work with people living with HIV and they always say, '*Oh how amazing, what an amazing job; it must be so difficult to see people suffering*'. That's before I even tell them that I am living with HIV.

Sometimes when I am doing education in a school about HIV, I feel like people look and think here is what happens to you if you do not take care of your sexual health and that I must have been living some risky lifestyle to get HIV or AIDS, as some people still insist on calling it. But how can you look after your sexual health if it's shameful to just go to the clinic, especially for women?

The basis for this pitying look or sideways glance can be a variety of things, but it always comes back to fear and ignorance about the subject and stigma and discrimination.

Misinformation is such a problem for people living with HIV. I would like to think that we have come a long way but when it comes to HIV, medication and treatment has come a long way, but the misconceptions and beliefs and lack of information still exist.

I am not sure what people are being told still but it is so very shocking when I hear the lack of up-to-date information; if people knew this information they would not only know how to prevent HIV, but they would also know that the myths are not true and that you can breathe the same air as somebody living with HIV. This was a question that I was once asked in a school.

The fear of HIV and what people still think it is associated with is totally shocking to me now that I am living with it, but to be honest if I had been given the appropriate information, I am not saying that it would not then have happened, that we will never know. Some of the biggest misconceptions and myths that I still hear are that HIV only affects gay men, you can catch it from toilets, and you can get it from kissing (none of these are true). Many people also think that it is drug users who are at the most at risk of HIV (not true). Some people still think that AIDS is something that you can catch and that once you have it, you are going to die. Also not true.

Preventing HIV transmission

The main route of transmission for HIV in the UK is through vaginal or anal unprotected sexual intercourse. To prevent HIV transmission, the best form of protection is condoms and these are available for free from sexual health clinics. There is now something called PrEP (pre-exposure prophylaxis). This is medication that can be taken to prevent the transmission of HIV. It does not, however, protect you from other sexually transmitted infections (STIs). Sexual health is as important as general health and if and when sexually active with or without protection, it is always good to get into the habit of regular testing. All tests are available online now, so you do not have to go to a clinic to be tested. Not having enough time is not a good enough excuse.

Some views are passed-on views, and we may not like to admit this. With time, it is changing. If you are being told something by somebody that either has more experience than you, or they are your elder or a senior member of staff, then why would you not believe what they are telling you? Again, this is not to blame them as somebody must have given them the information or opinion and they are just passing on what they think is correct knowledge. But this has to change. We cannot let outdated beliefs and lack of knowledge be the basis of people's knowledge going forward.

These misconceptions mean that I experience social exclusion and belong to a group of people who also experience this, and what for? Because one of the biggest misconceptions is that the people living with HIV are passing it on to others. Now this may seem a shock but it's not the people living well with HIV that are passing it on to others; it is the people that do not know their HIV status. It is the people that think it will not affect them; after all, why would it? – they are not gay or Black or transgender or from a third world country. How and why do people still not know that HIV does not discriminate? It is people that do.

One time at work I took a call from a man whose son had recently been diagnosed with HIV. He was ringing to check if he needed to get separate cutlery, plates etc and if there were any precautions he needed to take. Now you may be thinking, did someone really do that, but it is true and even worse than that is some people still think things like this. To be honest I do not think we can think badly of this man because the fear and ignorance that was instilled into society automatically made people think that this is what they had to do to protect themselves. Even I had stopped my family using my cups and plates when I was first diagnosed, even though I knew it couldn't be passed on this way.

Another common misconception is about saliva. I always see news reports about somebody being spat at and then they are waiting for the results of an HIV test. Even though it is truly disgusting to be spat at (and I do know), you are not going to become HIV positive; the media is just feeding us bad information.

Some of my more personal experiences of discrimination through misconceptions have been in health care settings. The first five years of my journey before starting ART (anti-retroviral therapy) I did experience some quite bad health scares which resulted in me being hospitalised. I was always put in a side room; I was constantly asked *'how did you get HIV?'* and treated differently. I had medication thrown into my room and my favourite: always scheduled as last of the day into surgery, just in case I infect the room and medical instruments.

I did not go back to my job after being diagnosed. I did not work again until I started volunteering, where I work now for an HIV charity. I have not experienced employment discrimination but have supported people who have. I will be honest in saying that despite the times I have thought about changing my job, the fear of discrimination (yes, despite all my knowledge and the Equality Act 2010) always stops me. I feel safe working in my own community. It may be just self-stigmatising but the fear is real. People seem to want to know when they are working with somebody with HIV, not that it makes any difference to their working day.

Society's overall vision of HIV is improving but it is still a constant battle. There is always a surprised face or two when I tell a room full of people that I am HIV positive and was diagnosed 15 years ago this March (2023). Or when you tell somebody what job you do, and they say *'oh, that must be so hard'*.

When I think back to my education, I do not remember any sexual health education that provided the information a person needs to help them navigate safely through learning about themselves sexually. I did not really think or know much about HIV until I was diagnosed. Younger generations tell me that it is still not taught in school. Sexual health is still deemed shameful, especially if you are a she/her. Labels are still being generated with negative tones. Why do labels need to be negative? With improved language use and friendlier terms, we can start to change the misconceptions and myths that surround HIV, and the drip of information will trickle down the correct information, challenging outdated stigma. HIV is often associated with risky behaviour, and this may be why people feel uncomfortable talking about it or providing a lesson based around sex. We do however need to think about it. As much as we need to change stigma and discrimination, we also need to end HIV transmission. This can be achieved through a combination of things and one of those is through education.

It's not all doom and gloom living with HIV but sometimes it's definitely not a walk in the park. All these challenges make it quite hard, and this makes it unbearable for some. That's why we still have people being diagnosed late (quite often having a worse outcome), or people being too ashamed to take medication. I was lucky that I found peer support early on in my journey. I was also lucky enough to be introduced to other women living with HIV. I think without this support my knowledge and outcome would not be where I am right now.

Women living with HIV

As a woman living with HIV, I do face different challenges from men. For example, I am six times more likely to experience cervical cancer and therefore have to have smears yearly. A public health study called Women and HIV (Terrence Higgins Trust, 2018) highlighted some of the key issues. Despite women being a third of people living with HIV in the UK, services are not addressing women's issues. The report highlighted a high level of unmet need. There is little knowledge around some of the health issues that women may experience compared to men and how this is affected by HIV. Women are more likely to experience violence because of their HIV status.

Women living with HIV have always been here and still our voices are not always heard; however, women living with HIV can have children just the same as anybody else. In the UK, the majority of babies born to women living with HIV are not born with HIV.

For more information on the experiences of women living with HIV, see:

www.tht.org.uk/our-work/our-campaigns/women-and-hiv-invisible-no-longer

www.gov.uk/government/publications/hiv-women-in-the-uk

https://rojavida.wordpress.com/portfolio/understanding-uu-for-women-living-with-hiv

The future

The day I was diagnosed, my life changed and yes it was not easy, but it made me see that we can turn things around. When I think back, I am not sure my life was that great anyway but that's all for different reasons. So along came this massive piece of news that suddenly gave me a different path.

My path became a lot better. I had lots of new people in my life; people that also understood how I felt. People who have become such an important part of who I am today. People who like me have experienced stigma and the feeling of being socially excluded.

I set a goal to become the manager of the centre where I began my peer-led journey; the goal was set, and I scored. I have now been the manager for over five years. I found a career which has offered me so many opportunities that I never had before. I learn so much and every day that does not stop. I keep on learning. Every day is a new day.

Living with HIV has given me so many more opportunities that I may not have otherwise had (that may sound crazy, I know) but it's true. To be honest, my generalised anxiety disorder gives me more problems, but it does not make people feel like they need to ask me, '*How did you get that?*' or step back from me worried that I may have touched something of theirs.

So, what are the positives for me living with HIV? Well, for one I have regular health checks which include the monitoring of organ functions and cholesterol, so I get a heads up on problems I may not know about until it is too late. I have met the most amazing people ever who are not just friends but extended family. I have been given opportunities that to be honest I do not think I would have ever experienced, and I have learnt. I have learnt so much, not just education stuff but how to live, how to be me and how to have a voice.

I chose to become an advocate and a voice for others. I chose to put myself out there and live as openly as possible with HIV and it was a good choice, one I do not regret in any way at all.

HIV does not define who I am as a person; it's just a small part of what makes me *me*.

I hope that by the year 2030 we can end HIV transmission and finally look towards a cure.

Further reading and viewing

We have shared a number of links throughout this chapter. If you would like to understand more about HIV, national and global targets or to understand more of the lived experience, there are a wide range of reports, websites, books and films you can access. We have shared a few here to get you started.

This is a great website: www.positivelyuk.org

National AIDS Trust are great for legislation, etc: www.nat.org.uk

This is a link to the apparent best 11 films about HIV/AIDS. *Dallas Buyers Club* and *Pride* are both good films: www.pride.com/hiv/2017/12/01/11-phenomenal-movies-about-hiv-and-aids

Terrence Higgins Trust can be accessed at: www.tht.org.uk

References

British Film Institute (1987) *AIDS: Iceberg*. [online] Available at: www.youtube.com/watch?v=sTB0HKAs0Eg (accessed 8 August 2022).

British Film Institute (1987) *AIDS: Monolith*. [online] Available at: www.youtube.com/watch?v=iroty5zw0Vw (accessed 8 August 2022).

Equality Act 2010 [online] Available at: www.legislation.gov.uk/ukpga/2010/15/contents (accessed 8 August 2022).

HIV.gov (2022) A Timeline of HIV and AIDS. [online] Available at: www.hiv.gov/hiv-basics/overview/history/hiv-and-aids-timeline (accessed 8 August 2022).

HIV i-Base (2021) U=U: Undetectable = Untransmittable. [online] Available at: https://i-base.info/u-equals-u (accessed 8 August 2022).

National AIDS Trust (2012) *HIV @ Work: Advice for Employees Living with HIV*. [online] Available at: www.nat.org.uk/sites/default/files/online-guides/Jul_2012_HIV%40Work_advice_for_employees_living_with_HIV-1_0_0.pdf (accessed 8 August 2022).

National AIDS Trust (2019) HIV in the UK Statistics. [online] Available at: www.nat.org.uk/about-hiv/hiv-statistics (accessed 8 August 2022).

National Institute for Health and Care Excellence (NICE) (2019) *NICE Impact Sexual Health*. [online] Available at: www.nice.org.uk/media/default/about/what-we-do/into-practice/measuring-uptake/niceimpact-sexual-health.pdf (accessed 8 August 2022).

Public Health England (2019) *Women and HIV in the United Kingdom: Data to End of December 2017*. [online] Available at: www.gov.uk/government/publications/hiv-women-in-the-uk (accessed 8 August 2022).

Roja Vida (nd) Understanding U=U for Women Living with HIV. [online] Available at: https://rojavida.wordpress.com/portfolio/understanding-uu-for-women-living-with-hiv (accessed 8 August 2022).

Terrence Higgins Trust (2018) *Women and HIV: Invisible No Longer*. [online] Available at: www.tht.org.uk/our-work/our-campaigns/women-and-hiv-invisible-no-longer (accessed 8 August 2022).

Terrence Higgins Trust (2022) HIV Statistics: Statistics about HIV in the UK, Including How Many People Are Currently Living with HIV. [online] Available at: www.tht.org.uk/hiv-and-sexual-health/about-hiv/hiv-statistics (accessed 9 August 2022).

UK Health Security Agency (2021) *HIV Testing, New HIV Diagnoses, Outcomes and Quality of Care for People Accessing HIV Services: 2021 Report.* [online] Available at: https://assets.publishing.service.gov.uk/government/uploads/system/uploads/attachment_data/file/1037215/hiv-2021-report.pdf (accessed 8 August 2022).

UNAIDS (2022) 90-90-90: An Ambitious Treatment Target to Help End the AIDS Epidemic. [online] Available at: www.unaids.org/en/resources/909090 (accessed 9 August 2022).

University of Sunderland (2022) Positive Allies. [online] Available at: www.sunderland.ac.uk/more/positive-allies (accessed 8 August 2022).

Chapter 9 | Being in prison

Myka Wilshire and Mel Hughes

When I was 19 years old, I went to prison for a driving offence. This wasn't my first time in prison; however, this time I was pregnant with my first child and was given a six-month custodial sentence for driving while disqualified.

During my pregnancy I had to be taken to the local maternity hospital in Bristol for my scans. This was, to date, up there with one of my most shameful, harrowing and humiliating experiences. When arriving at the hospital, both my wrists were handcuffed and then I was handcuffed with a chain attached to a prison guard with a second guard escorting us. We presented to the reception at the hospital. No private room had been arranged, nor even discussed and I was seated in the main waiting area of the maternity clinic where it was packed with families. Children playing in the play area were beckoned by their parents and not allowed to play. The scene in front of them, I understand, was quite disturbing and for all they knew I was a serial killer. The looks of horror and disgust, especially as I was also pregnant, were so intense. I felt humiliated and ashamed and quite honestly felt I had no right to be a parent in that moment.

During the scan, which arguably was one of the most precious moments of my life, I was handcuffed to the bed and spoken to in such a matter-of-fact way; no compassion, or willingness to understand what I was going through was evident, all I felt was judged.

My mum and my sister had rightfully contacted the prison on numerous occasions and informed them that they wanted to be with me during my scans. This was rejected and none of us were ever informed when my scans would be due to the risk of me absconding. This risk was not based on any evidence or previous intelligence and was just an assumption. My family were not able to be part of such a life-changing period of time.

Luckily for me, on my second scan after hearing about my trauma of the first experience, my mum and sister, who are very strong willed, waited at the prison all day for several days for the transportation car to pick me up due to them having a rough idea what week the scan was due. They followed the car to the hospital and when they arrived and saw me sat in the usual waiting area full of people demanded that I was treated appropriately and given some privacy to wait. I can't tell you how grateful I was and am to this day for their love and support and that they had to do what they did to ensure I was treated like a human being and not a convict on display to be humiliated.

Pregnant women and prison

In May 2022, there were 3221 women in prison in England and Wales (Ministry of Justice, 2022). About 600 pregnant women enter a UK prison each year and about 50 are in prison at any one time (Epstein et al, 2021).

Concern continues to be raised regarding the quality of care received by pregnant women while in prison. One in five appointments with midwives and 40 per cent of outpatient appointments are missed (Abbott, 2020), often because prison staff are not available to take women to the appointment. Women are locked in their cells at night when there are no on-site midwives or doctors. This is despite women in prison being more likely to have high-risk pregnancies (Abbott, 2020). Analysis in 2017–18 by the Nuffield Trust (2019) found that roughly one in ten pregnant women gave birth either in their prison cell or on route to hospital.

Epstein et al (2021) argue that imprisonment for pregnant women is not necessary and highlight that it is no longer permitted in 11 other countries where alternatives including house arrest, electronic monitoring and probation are used instead.

During the sentence my family were able to visit me in prison; however, there were no specialist staff such as midwives or health visitors available to talk to. So, while pregnant in prison with my first child at the age of 19, I had no clue what was happening to me and no one to talk to outside of my family through usual visiting times or phone calls with limited spends.

During this period, my dad was in hospital terminally ill with HIV that had now become AIDS. At the beginning of the sentence, I was advised that he would be unlikely to survive 24 hours and so anxiously waited every day to hear the rattling of the chaplain's keys to inform me he had died. Thankfully my dad held on and on the day of release from prison, my mum and sister picked me up and took me straight to the hospital. I managed to spend 20 minutes with him. He knew that both the baby and I were safe and well and then when I left that day, he died shortly after.

When sentenced in prison, you can only spend a small set amount of money per week on canteen, phone etc. This was not increased to support me with additional phone credit to ease my stress and anxiety during my time of pregnancy, with my dad dying, nor for me to buy additional food that I could keep down. My cravings and appetite had changed so much that I was struggling to eat many food types that the prison provided, and they were unable to change this for me.

I do appreciate I had committed a crime and needed to take full responsibility for this. I was in prison for a driving while disqualified offence, and while I understand this could have been devastating to someone if I had crashed, no direct harm was caused to anyone.

Although pregnant, I felt like I had lost my right to be a parent. This was a direct result of my environment and the people around me. The systemic messaging was that I had no rights. No midwives, health visitors, no social workers, no family support workers; absolutely no acknowledgement by the prison system that I was pregnant. The system simply doesn't acknowledge the impact of this and doesn't provide the resources to support you through this process. This was compounded by a lack of empathy and compassion by any of the staff in the prison or hospital. I felt judged, alone, ashamed, hopeless and unsupported to change. How was I supposed to change if there was no one to support and guide me to do so?

Women in prison

Over half of women in prison have experienced emotional, physical or sexual abuse as a child; around one in three have experienced being in care as a child; almost two in three report being survivors of domestic abuse; seven out of ten have mental ill health. Approximately three in five women in prison are mothers with children under the age of 18. Ninety-five per cent of children have to leave their own home when their mother goes to prison as the mother is often the primary caregiver (Women in Prison, 2022).

Levels of self-harm in women's prisons reached record levels in 2020. There were 11,988 incidents of self-harm compared to 7670 in 2016. Women made up 22 per cent of all self-harm incidents in 2020, despite making up only 4 per cent of the prison population (Prison Reform Trust, 2021). Written evidence from the National Women's Prisons Health and Social Care Review in 2021 reported that high numbers of women in prison have complex histories of trauma, which are often left undiagnosed and untreated.

More than three out of five women are sent to prison for sentences less than six months (Ministry of Justice, 2022), most commonly for theft. In the majority of cases, they are considered low risk to society.

Chief executive of the national charity Women in Prison, Kate Paradine, said: 'There is another way – when women are supported in the community, they have better access to care and can tackle the issues that sweep

> *them into crime in the first place, like trauma, domestic abuse and poverty'* (Summers, 2022).
>
> The use of community sentences, however, has dropped by two-thirds since 2010 (Prison Reform Trust, 2021).

For the first year of my son's life after my release, I did my best to be a great mum and had an incredible bond with my son. However, it was apparent that with all the will in the world, my addiction was stronger than anything and I again started to use crack and heroin. For some time, I managed to keep everything functioning with the support of my family, who at this time had no idea of my drug use. When my son was approximately two years old, my mum and sister moved to Australia. As my addiction progressed so did my criminality, which again resulted in me being put in prison, again for driving while disqualified.

When I was arrested, I was in Devon. I had my son with me; he was about three years old at this time. The police advised me that I wouldn't be given bail and that in fact I would be taken to court the following day with a view to remanding me in prison.

My son was taken to the house of my boyfriend's parents (which I did not know at the time), who looked after him for a few days while my mum arranged to fly over from Australia to pick him up and take him back with her.

When I got to prison it was a nightmare to find out what was happening with my son. Due to my family being in Australia, I wasn't allowed to call there with my one phone call. I was not informed where my son was until I managed to get my numbers added to my phone account, which took four days. I was then able to call Australia and was advised that my mum was on route to the UK to collect my son and that he was safe with my boyfriends' parents.

When my mum arrived and collected my son, she booked a prison visit and brought him to see me just before her flight back to Australia with him. It was a hard visit with no clue when I would see him again; however, I knew he was in the best place. During this sentence, there again were no additional arrangements to accommodate contact, taking into consideration the time differences, which rarely enabled phone calls due to lock-up times. Again, it is so hard to be in this environment and not have people to support you through this process.

When I came out of prison this time, my family made it clear that I needed to do some work on myself prior to them being willing to let me have my son return to me. During the next few years, I made many attempts at being abstinent and in recovery, which enabled me to have my son return to me. However, these attempts seemed short-lived as I continued to have co-dependent, unhealthy relationships with no clue that this was a recurring cycle.

Women and substance use

Research has consistently shown that women experience drug use differently to men. Women are more likely to be introduced to drugs by a partner, to start using drugs as a coping mechanism, rather than recreationally, and they progress to problematic use more quickly (Tuchman, 2010).

In a study by Canfield et al (2021, p 1), the risk to women was shown to be greater if they had children. They found that mothers in their study '*were more likely to be young, experience housing problems, use opioids and/or crack-cocaine in the past 28 days and experience lifetime domestic violence victimizations*'.

Intimate partner violence has been shown to be a predictor of problematic drug use in women (Ogden et al, 2022) as has traumatic stress, in particular high-impact trauma such as childhood sexual violence, physical abuse and neglect (Hien et al, 2005).

Despite this, women are significantly under-represented in treatment services. This is often seen to be due to a lack of services designed and centred on their needs (We Are With You, 2021) and women who are mothers fearing that their children will be removed if they disclose their drug use (Canfield et al, 2021).

Evidence shows however that those in treatment do better than those who are not. '*Drug treatment protects families. It helps parents to stabilise their lives and look after children better*' (NTA, 2012, p 2).

My last prison sentence was in 2008/09, when I was convicted of possession of class A drugs. I had just had my second son, who had been removed from me at three months old and was now in foster care. My eldest son was now living with my aunty and uncle, and I was not allowed to have any contact with him at this time due to my drug use. My youngest son's dad was extremely abusive and quite honestly I was terrified of him. My case was being held at MARAC and prison seemed like a safe place to be and a welcome relief.

MARAC

A MARAC is a Multi-Agency Risk Assessment Conference where information is shared on the highest-risk domestic abuse cases. Key services, including health, child protection, probation, domestic violence and police, share information and agree an action plan to safeguard the victim (SafeLives, 2022).

During this period, court proceedings were taking place to look at the future for my youngest son. Due to my family living in Australia and the proposal of taking him out the country, this added complications to the process. His dad did not agree to this and instead decided that he would fight for custody. In the beginning he tried this himself and then, once he realised he would not be successful, bullied his mother to try and gain custody.

During this process I was clearly having a mental breakdown. I didn't ever know what was going on. I was so terrified that his dad would find a way to have him and that my son would end up dead due to his dad's violent nature. I felt so alone and unable to manage with limited contact with my family in Australia and no one to talk to, to advocate or to liaise with children's social care. I wholeheartedly accepted that I could not protect my child and that he shouldn't be with me; however, I was not included or communicated with effectively to enable me to manage my fears that were crippling me. I was losing my mind and felt broken, and no one seemed to notice or care. The prison's response to this was to give me more medication to sedate me. No one ever came to talk to me to even ask what I needed or to explore ways to support me. I just needed someone to communicate what was happening and to reassure me that my son would be protected.

There were points that I would kick off in frustration due to the lack of communication. I didn't know what was going on with my son, the court proceedings, if I would see him or what the processes were. This was all while it only being a few months since giving birth. My body and hormones were still trying to settle and there was no thought or consideration to what my needs were. On a couple of occasions when I kicked off by slamming doors or shouting at officers, the response to this was to give me a punishment by putting me on basic. This means that you are locked in your cell for 23 hours a day, with your TV removed and left on your own with just your thinking and emotions to deal with. I do not understand how this feels a viable response to my frustrated behaviour because of the trauma I was feeling.

Support for women in prison

In 2018, the government published *Gender Specific Standards to Improve Health and Wellbeing for Women in Prison in England* (Public Health England, 2018) and the Female Offender Strategy (Ministry of Justice, 2018) for England and Wales.

The Standards highlighted the need for a system approach. This included:

» preventing offending by tackling the wider determinants of health and supporting upstream prevention of substance misuse, violence, unemployment and exclusion from school;

» ensuring that while in prison women have access to high-quality health and care services to support improvements to their mental health, substance misuse and general health;

» developing an environment in prison which gives opportunities for women to improve their health by improving nutrition and encouraging participation in physical activity;

» giving adequate support to women who have children within the prison in mother and baby units, and those who are separated from their children;

» ensuring that support is available for women who leave prison in terms of housing, training and employment opportunities, appropriate access to social welfare and other benefits if applicable, continuation of treatment and referral into appropriate community services.

In the Female Offender Strategy, the government highlighted the need for early intervention, community-based solutions and the need for more effective and decent custody for women who do have to be in prison.

Three years on, the Prison Reform Trust reported in 2021 that '*Progress has been slow – only 31 of 65 commitments in the Female Offender Strategy have been fully achieved. Where commitments have been met through publication of guidance or instructions there is little or no information on whether they are having the desired impact. The strategy is not backed up by clear and comprehensive measures of success.*'

The three-day court hearing regarding the care of my son was set for two days after my release from prison, which I would attend. There was no preparation for this. I had no idea what to expect. I was terrified to see my ex there and again no one to talk this through with.

My youngest son's social worker did her best by me and in fact brought my son up to visit me on one occasion. I felt that although she was clearly there to ensure my son was protected and his best interests were the priority, she showed me compassion and understanding, albeit she was very honest, which at times was hard. I still have a special place in my heart for this lady. She did everything in her power to protect my son when I couldn't, even through especially challenging times with his father, who often intimidated and made threats to anyone who tried to get in his way. This included her.

Was the custodial sentence proportionate? In light of the impact on myself and more importantly my children, I would say *no*. It compounded trauma with trauma. There was certainly no rehabilitation or therapy. What there was were more traumatic experiences that reaffirmed to me I was a rubbish person that would never change and that my children would be better off without me. Hopeless.

I grew up in a household with a dad who was a drug addict and alcoholic who died of AIDS as a result of his active addiction and spent all his adult life in and out of prison and a mum who had undiagnosed (at the time) bipolar disorder. While I knew that I was loved and my mum did an incredible job as a single parent, my childhood was dysfunctional. How was I supposed to know how to change a spiral-ling negative pattern of behaviour without the support and guidance to do so? I was a child having a child and not knowing what to do. I had gone down a destructive path since I was 13 years of age and needed help to change course before I dragged my child/children down the same path. I always remember thinking '*I love my dad so much, but I will never do what he has done to me to my children when I have them*'. Well, I did…

The system in my view is punitive and archaic. As a woman in prison, I did not feel that there was adequate support for mothers and that in fact there is an undertone of a '*you gave up your right to be a mother when you committed an offence*' attitude. There was no support to help you navigate the trauma of losing children, either through family or court proceedings. There was a family day offered twice a year that you could apply for, but it wasn't guaranteed. On top of this, there was no provision to rehabilitate from specific traumas like domestic abuse, including sexual abuse. Instead, what was avail-able was to be prescribed multiple antidepressant and antipsychotic medications to keep us sedated instead of using the time to address some of these issues. During my time in prison, I managed to get myself addicted to various medications that the prison prescribed to me. I believed that I needed these to live. This was just not the case and in fact since being in recovery for coming up to 11 years, I have not needed to take any medication to manage my emotions or mental well-being.

I didn't grow up aspiring to be a drug addict or to go to prison. I was a gymnast that had a back accident. My life in prison as a drug addict who lost her children and caused harm to all her loved ones wasn't my dream. I believe it was a result of going down a wrong path as a teenager and being unable to find the way to turn it around.

Children experiencing parental substance use

Children experiencing parental substance use are at higher risk of developing substance use disorders themselves (Biederman et al, 2000; Meulewaeter et al, 2022).

Meulewaeter et al (2022) highlight the central role of feelings of loneliness, isolation and belonging in both childhood and adulthood. Three themes were identified from their analysis:

1. loneliness and childhood trauma and neglect;

2. stigma and the self;

3. the role of social connection in substance use and recovery.

They suggest that experience of stigma as a child regarding a substance-using parent can contribute to a lack of positive self-esteem and inter-personal difficulties for children for which substance use can be seen as a solution.

I relate to all three of the following themes.

Loneliness and childhood trauma and neglect

Loneliness and lack of connection to anyone was a massive part of my childhood. I didn't actually feel a sense of connection with myself, let alone others. Due to the lack of structure or routine in the family home, I was never sure when my parents would be around, what the mood would be like when they were (this was extremely volatile at times and unpredictable), who they would have with them and if this would be a positive experience or a negative one.

I was always aware from a very young age not to mention what was going on at home with anyone as this could cause problems if teachers, social workers etc found out. I definitely felt feelings of shame and embarrassment about what my family life looked like and longed for a 'normal family home'. Presence, consistency and routine.

I experienced physical abuse and emotional and material neglect. I am able to see now that my parents loved me greatly and were just doing the best that they could with what they had. In turn, I see the similarities with my experiences and the experiences of my own children. While I was not physically abusive, I too neglected my children emotionally.

I also see how the feelings of abandonment and rejection played out in my life. I put a protective wall around me to not be vulnerable as everyone will leave me and let me down anyway.

Stigma and the self

During my childhood it was normal to lie to everyone, sometimes to hide what was going on but also it was normal to lie for my parents. It was normalised to lie and to live in a false reality. The feelings of low self-worth go back as far as I remember, blaming myself for my dad often going missing for weeks, months and at times years with no idea why. My mum either being in bed for days or out partying for days.

The shame of how poor we were and the conditions we were living in – dirty clothes, poor hygiene etc – massively impacted how I felt about myself. As I got older, into my early teenage years, I felt comfortable to seek out other people that were not living a 'normal family life'. This way I didn't feel as embarrassed and ashamed. I gravitated to people drinking, taking drugs and committing crimes. When I was around them, I didn't feel different. I felt accepted and included. There was, for the first time, a sense of connection and community that I was part of.

The role of social connection in substance use and recovery

Drugs and alcohol in the home were part of the norm in my childhood and the risk associated with that were also part of normal life; therefore, I didn't understand the severity of this risk.

While my mum predominantly had alcohol, cannabis and at times cocaine in the house due to her partying lifestyle, my dad was an alcoholic and an IV heroin and crack cocaine user. I have many memories of seeing drugs in his house. My dad also sold drugs, so drug users were always about. They often bought me sweets and spoilt me. I felt cared for by loads of people in the drug-using community so to me I felt like I was the lucky one. When I consider how I felt about this and how normalised it all was, I realise that I felt like my dad's life was like the bright lights of Las Vegas. It was fun, exciting and I didn't feel isolated or alone. It was an attractive proposition to me. This seems insane, especially in light of my dad having HIV and essentially what was then a death sentence as a result of his drug use.

Social exclusion

I don't feel socially excluded now I am in recovery; however, it would be easy for people with my experiences to feel socially excluded. I think that due to my passion and drive to challenge oppression and to promote positive change, I haven't allowed the system to exclude me. I am lucky that I now work in drug and alcohol treatment services, who welcome people with lived experiences. I do feel that other areas of the health and social care sector may not be so inclusive.

I believe that having had experience of adversity in childhood has made me very driven. Often people like myself can be high achievers, that never feeling enough so they are always looking at 'what next'. It's almost like proving to yourself that you are good enough.

Throughout my career, I have always had to disclose my convictions due to the work I do. For every position I have been recruited to, I have had to go through a risk assessment with my manager, going through each offence and describing why I did it and how I feel about it now. This is quite a humiliating process as I have 58 convictions and have to discuss them all. I do however understand that working with vulnerable people requires robust safeguards to be in place so agree that this process needs to be done.

Today

Today, I am 11 years abstinent from all mood/mind-altering substances. I have both of my children in my life and am a fantastic parent. I am a manager of a drug and alcohol project and spend much of my time both inside and outside of work trying to challenge social exclusion to inform change. I am passionate about positive change and a system that supports and promotes this.

I would like to say that I managed this change as a result of the criminal justice system; unfortunately, I didn't.

The change started when a drug and alcohol worker in the community had so much belief and faith in me, that I could do anything I wanted to, when I was absolutely hopeless. That worker would talk me through all my amazing attributes and look at what areas I was really struggling with and what support I needed. I felt supported, guided, understood. I was told it was ok; I had been ill and that it wasn't because I was a bad person. I was told that they would walk beside me on the long road of recovery and that change was hard but achievable, and that I was worth it.

References

Abbott, L (2020) The Impact of Imprisonment on Pregnant Women and Their Unborn Children. [online] Available at: www.youtube.com/watch?v=ydrISNYoECk (accessed 8 August 2022).

Biederman, J, Faraone, S V, Monuteaux, M C and Feighner, J A (2000) Patterns of Alcohol and Drug Use in Adolescents Can Be Predicted by Parental Substance Use Disorders. *Pediatrics*, 106(4): 792–7.

Canfield, M, Norton, S, Downs, J and Gilchrist, G (2021) Parental Status and Characteristics of Women in Substance Use Treatment Services: Analysis of Electronic Patient Records. *Journal of Substance Abuse Treatment*, 127.

Epstein, R, Brown, G and Garcia De Frutos, M (2021) *Why are Pregnant Women in Prison?* Coventry: Coventry University. [online] Available at: www.coventry.ac.uk/globalassets/media/global/08-new-research-sect ion/cawr/pregnant-women-in-prison-a4-final-report.pdf (accessed 8 August 2022).

Hien, D, Cohen, L and Campbell, A (2005) Is Traumatic Stress a Vulnerability Factor for Women with Substance Use Disorders? *Clinical Psychology Review*, 25(6): 813–23

House of Commons Library (2021) *UK Prison Population Statistics.* October 2021. [online] Available at: https://researchbriefings.files.parliament.uk/documents/SN04334/SN04334.pdf (accessed 8 August 2022).

Meulewaeter, F, De Schauwer, E, De Pauw, S S W and Vanderplasschen, W (2022) "I Grew Up Amidst Alcohol and Drugs": A Qualitative Study on the Lived Experiences of Parental Substance Use Among Adults Who Developed Substance Use Disorders Themselves. *Frontiers in Psychiatry*, 13: 768802.

Ministry of Justice (2018) Female Offender Strategy. [online] Available at: https://assets.publishing.serv ice.gov.uk/government/uploads/system/uploads/attachment_data/file/719819/female-offender-strat egy.pdf (accessed 8 August 2022).

Ministry of Justice (2022) May 2022 Prison Population Bulletin. [online] Available at: www.gov.uk/gov ernment/publications/prison-population-figures-2022 (accessed 8 August 2022).

National Treatment Agency for Substance Misuse (NTA) (2012) *Parents with Drug Problems: How Treatment Helps Families.* [online] Available at: www.nta.nhs.uk/uploads/families2012vfinali.pdf (accessed 8 August 2022).

National Women's Prisons Health and Social Care Review (2021). Written Evidence. [online] Available at: https://committees.parliament.uk/writtenevidence/36773/pdf (accessed 8 August 2022).

Nuffield Trust (2019) Pregnancy and Childbirth in Prison: What Do We Know? [online] Available at: www.nuffieldtrust.org.uk/news-item/pregnancy-and-childbirth-in-prison-what-do-we-know (accessed 14 September 2022).

Ogden, S N, Dichter, M E and Bazzi, A R (2022) Intimate Partner Violence as a Predictor of Substance Use Outcomes Among Women: A Systematic Review. *Addictive Behaviours*, 127: 107214.

Prison Reform Trust (2021) *Why Focus on Reducing Women's Imprisonment? England and Wales: July 2021*. Briefing. [online] Available at: www.prisonreformtrust.org.uk/wp-content/uploads/old_files/Documents/Women/Why%20women%202021%20briefing%20FINAL.pdf (accessed 8 August 2022).

Public Health England (2018) *Gender Specific Standards to Improve Health and Wellbeing for Women in Prison in England*. [online] Available at: https://assets.publishing.service.gov.uk/government/uploads/system/uploads/attachment_data/file/687146/Gender_specific_standards_for_women_in_prison_to_improve_health_and_wellbeing.pdf (accessed 8 August 2022).

SafeLives (2022) Frequently Asked Questions: Multi-Agency Risk Assessment Conferences (MARAC). [online] Available at: https://safelives.org.uk/sites/default/files/resources/MARAC%20FAQs%20General%20FINAL.pdf (accessed 8 August 2022).

Summers, H (2022) Call to Stop Jailing Pregnant Women in England After Baby Dies in Prison Toilet. *The Guardian*, 16 January. [online] Available at: www.theguardian.com/society/2022/jan/16/call-to-stop-jailing-pregnant-women-in-england-after-baby-dies-in-prison-toilet (accessed 8 August 2022).

Tuchman E (2010) Women and Addiction: The Importance of Gender Issues in Substance Abuse Research. *Journal of Addictive Diseases* 29(2): 127–38.

We Are With You (2021) *A System Designed for Women? Understanding the Barriers Women Face in Accessing Drug Treatment and Support Services*. [online] Available at: www.wearewithyou.org.uk/documents/43/A_System_designed_for_women.pdf (accessed 8 August 2022).

Women in Prison (2022) Key Facts. [online] Available at: https://womeninprison.org.uk/about/key-facts (accessed 8 August 2022).

Chapter 10 | Being a Gypsy

Lisa-Marie Price and Peter Unwin

This is me… one voice speaking out against social exclusion of the Gypsy, Roma and Traveller communities.

My name is Lisa-Marie, 20 years of age. I belong to a large, yet loving, family with my mam, Kimberley, at the centre of it. She is my role model and supported me with my aspirations. Being born into the Gypsy/Traveller community, my life was already written out for me. But I did not want the life which was expected of me. At my current age – traditionally, I should be settled with a husband and children; however, I am not. You are wondering why… is there something wrong with me, why am I not married? To be honest I could not see myself being settled at an early age and not having experienced what life has to offer. I was torn. My parents were torn. Do I stay and settle, or do I break the mould and become an individual? What will the repercussions be?

I want to highlight that there is not one single person to blame for the social exclusion or discrimination we experience. It is the lack of awareness and, in some cases ignorance, while platforms such as television and social media continually produce negative and discriminatory images and stories about my community.

Origins of Gypsy, Roma and Traveller peoples

Gypsy, Roma and Travellers have been oppressed and excluded from mainstream societies across the world for thousands of years. Contemporary media and government actions continue to oppress these cultures to the present day, in the UK as well as abroad. Debate continues about the origins of Gypsies, Roma and Travellers, who are not from Egypt, despite what many people think. Most scholars believe that Gypsies, Roma and Travellers originated from India back in the tenth century and subsequently spread westwards. The Romani languages spoken among the diverse cultures bear great similarities with the ancient Indian language of Sanskrit. The two short documentaries below are excellent introductions to the complex origins of Gypsies, Roma and Travellers. The first video, 'Roads From the Past' (Travellers' Times Films, 2019), concentrates on the British/ Irish context, whereas the second one, 'Gypsies, Roma and Travellers – An

Animated History' (Open Society Foundations, 2013), traces the migration westwards from India in the tenth century, providing many examples of social exclusion and even slavery along the way. Much Gypsy, Roma and Traveller history is oral and therefore can be lost over time.

I often wonder why the media are so discriminatory because not all of us are bad people, but in fact respectable, decent, clean people who bring no harm to others. In current times, it has been encouraging to see Gypsy/Traveller women discussing their issues, stories and views more through social media (our menfolk rarely get involved in such discussions, gender roles often being quite separate). This has had a positive impact on the way in which women are viewed within our cultures, and that how having a voice is important. It is important not to generalise about our communities as they are often quite different, as the above videos demonstrate. The term *GRT* is often used to lump us together, but this term is really just an administrative convenience that we prefer not to use. In the UK, you will find English Gypsies, Welsh Gypsies, Scottish Gypsy Travellers, Irish Travellers, Roma, Boaters, Showmen and New Age Travellers, all of whom have quite distinct mores and ways of life. What we do share, sadly, is the experience of being socially excluded and 'othered'.

Cultures within cultures

English Gypsies, Irish Travellers, Welsh Gypsies, Scottish Gypsy Travellers and Roma enjoy ethnic minority status under the Equality Act 2010, although many people in those communities are unaware of their rights under such legislation (Unwin et al, 2020). The use of language to describe these cultures and ethnicities can be confusing. It is best practice, for both the public and professionals, to ask individuals and communities how they would like to be known. Some communities use the term *Romany* or *Traveller* to describe their culture, and these terms can variously be used in respect of the above groups. In Europe, the term *Roma* is used for a whole range of cultures, and the term *Gypsy* can be seen as an insult rather than a heritage to be proud of, as I am. Some European counties, such as Hungary and Romania, still openly discriminate against Roma in terms of housing, educational and work opportunities. Many Roma have migrated in recent decades to what they see as more liberal counties; although, as my story will tell, the UK is not actually so liberal.

Many Gypsy, Roma and Traveller people 'pass', that is, deny their heritage and try to act as if they were someone else. This type of behaviour is due to a fear of discrimination and oppression; even successful professionals sometimes do not reveal their true identity until they have become successful or reached senior positions. Even people who work for Gypsy, Roma and Traveller organisations sometimes only reveal their ethnicity at work and hide it from their neighbours.

Mental ill health

There are very high levels of mental ill health in many Gypsy, Roma and Traveller communities. A recent study in Ireland (All Ireland Traveller Health Study, 2010) reported suicide rates among Irish Traveller men to be some seven times higher than the national average, with suicide accounting for 11 per cent of all deaths in the Traveller communities. Greenfields and Rogers (2020) drew a connection between relentless negative media stereotypes and the troubling levels of mental ill health across Gypsy, Roma and Traveller communities, in a report tellingly titled *Hate: 'As Regular as Rain'.*

Among some communities there is a distrust of health services and of mainstream authorities in general; the historical realities of centuries of oppression, slavery, being experimented upon and killed in their thousands by the Nazis in the Holocaust leave fears that run deep. There are some developing mental health services being run by communities for communities (eg One Call Away and the Showmen's Mental Health Awareness Charity), which are encouraging signs of community empowerment, and the suicide rate scandal actually made it onto *BBC News* (Page and McGlinchey, 2022) in 2022, suggesting that there is a new interest in the mental health crisis among Gypsy, Roma and Traveller communities.

Reflective activity

What do you think could be done to help improve mental ill health in Gypsy, Roma and Traveller communities?

Just imagine the long-term effect of day-to-day discrimination on a young community member who faces discrimination at school, on the street, on TV programmes, on social media and even from the UK government. The passing of the recent Police, Crime, Sentencing and Courts Act 2022 criminalised over-night stopping, thus eliminating part of a culture which has been part of our heritage forever.

Imagine living in an Irish Traveller community where you would know so many friends and family, often young people, who had taken their own lives. How might this affect your own mental health?

When I was younger, life seemed so simple. At home I created many of my memories with my mam, dad and brother. I attended primary school like other people, yet I would be singled out by parents and children, the latter telling me '*I cannot play with you; you are different*'. Little did I know this was only the beginning of the discrimination and exclusion I would endure due to my culture. Primary school was tolerable; I attended well and gained as much basic knowledge as I could. When asked if I wanted to attend high school, I immediately said '*Yes*'. I loved learning about new things and being able to talk about them when I get home. Deciding what high school to attend was easy as my non-Traveller friends were attending my same-choice school, making me feel more at ease. On starting high school, I kept my culture away 8:30am–3:00pm, to keep any form of bullying at bay. This was exhausting, and when snide comments were made, I would be filled with anger, but did nothing. This continued until Year 8 where I had finally had enough, and when I would be asked '*Are you a Gypsy?*' I would reply '*Yes*'. It was such a huge relief, like a weight lifted off my shoulders. It was only after that I would have to face the consequences. Some people were curious and wanted to know more, asking questions with reference to programmes such as *Big Fat Gypsy Weddings* originally shown on Channel 4 TV.

Negative **stereotyping**

The *Big Fat Gypsy Weddings* Channel 4 series promoted negative stereo-types of Gypsy/Traveller culture, with young girls being portrayed in very sexualised ways. The other impression given was that all Gypsies have huge amounts of money to spend, whereas the reality is that many Gypsy, Roma and Traveller people live in, or near, poverty, especially since traditional forms of employment (scrap dealing, agricultural labour, horse trading) have dried up. Other recent programmes such as Ed Stafford's documen-tary *60 Days with the Gypsies* (Channel 4, 2022) shape the image of all Gypsy, Roma and Travellers in most people's minds and, to date, our com-munities have not had the voice to effectively counter these discriminatory approaches. With the government passing discriminatory legislation, as exemplified in the Police, Crime, Sentencing and Courts Act 2022, it could be argued that the government themselves support such discriminatory views, and that their real plan is to assimilate us and eradicate our lifestyles and heritage.

Reflective activity

Watch one of the many episodes of *Big Fat Gypsy Weddings*, which are still available across the internet, and see if you agree or not with the views of *Guardian* journalist John Plunkett about the long-term harm, racism and bullying that stems from such mainstream portrayals of Traveller culture (www.theguardian.com/media/2012/oct/16/big-fat-gypsy-weddings-bullying-travellers)

Discrimination against Gypsy, Roma and Traveller communities has been described as '*the last acceptable form of racism*' (Traveller Movement, 2017). The comedian Jimmy Carr has been criticised by Gypsy, Roma and Traveller organisations and professional associations (eg British Association of Social Workers, 2022) for his Netflix show which included the 'joke' that the only positive thing about the Holocaust was the thousands of Gypsies who were killed. The audience laughed uproariously. Carr has since refused to apologise, and his 2022 nationwide tour went ahead.

Would that have happened had he told a similar 'joke' about Black people, or gay people, or Muslims?

I did not mind being asked questions concerning my ethnicity, as it shows country people (we use the terms *country people* or *gorgers* to describe non-Gypsy, Roma and Traveller people) are wanting to know more, and to be inclusive, ensuring they do not cause offence. On the other hand, this openness fuelled other people's agendas to bully me. Name-calling, online bullying and physical bullying all took place regularly throughout my time in high school through to university. I am one of the very few Gypsies to ever make it to university, partly because of cultural tradition, but also because of a fear of discrimination and the fact that many Gypsy and Traveller children do badly at primary school, and many do not finish secondary school.

Traditionally this would largely have been because jobs were lined up for the boys at an early age and girls were needing to be prepared for a young marriage, child rearing and home-making duties. Nowadays, in contrast to some of the anti-Gypsism views about promiscuity and criminality in our cultures, the main reason many parents do not want their girls, in particular, to attend secondary school is because they see teenage school life as a rather unsavoury culture with bullying, promiscuity and substance abuse.

I have certainly found it difficult to fit in within gorgers and to make friends, and despite attending a small and welcoming university, the University of Worcester, 'fitting in' has been difficult, despite achieving academic success. I do not really talk about my time at university when back home with family and friends, because they cannot relate to it, and I do not wish to come across as 'better than them'. I am not; I just chose a different path and want to keep the best of both cultures. I think this blending of cultures is important, especially as the old Gypsy trades and lifestyles fade away and the travelling life is lessening (some 80 per cent of Gypsies and Travellers now live in houses and on sites – very few travel all year round). The fuss made in the press and on social media when groups of Travellers park up on a common or wasteland and leave behind a mess often involves Irish Travellers travelling for work or visiting families. Local councils have repeatedly failed to build permanent or transit sites for Travellers and traditional stopping places are often now barred for entry or have disappeared under new development. The councils do not usually provide any toileting or refuse disposal facilities and, as Ed Stafford's recent documentary (Channel 4, 2022) showed, current regulations prohibit anyone without a local van permit from taking their refuse to a council tip.

What about the headlines we never see? – 'Gypsies Park on Common for Two Days; Nothing Is Stolen, and They Left the Place Just as They Found It' – those stories do not get reported. It is the same with the world-famous Appleby Horse Fair in Cumbria where the Gypsy, Roma and Traveller organisations always clean up the camping fields with a special team, but the TV cameras never wait for those shots – they film the very worst images possible, including youths fighting and claiming horses are maltreated. Any large gathering in the UK attracts refuse and trouble elements; look at what goes on at festivals – the waste and mess – but that does not result in discrimination against festival goers. As a Gypsy woman whose family business is running an equestrian centre, why would we mistreat a horse? The opposite is true – we love and pamper our animals, which also makes good business sense. Furthermore, many of the animals with which we work are rescue horses and ponies from outside of our community.

Reflective activity

'Antigypsism' is a word you may not be familiar with and, just like ageism or disablism, it describes approaches and attitudes to certain sets of people in negative stereotyped ways. The concept of *aversive racism* is another phrase you may not have heard. It was first used by Dovidio and Gaertner (1986) and has been used more recently by Allen and Hulmes (2021) in their study around the high numbers of Gypsy, Roma and Traveller children taken into state care. 'Aversive racism' is when a person states that they believe in equal opportunities and welcome diversity but, inside, they are 'averse' or 'opposed' to the idea. These are false people who live their lives as a lie.

Ask your friends and family how they would react if planning permission was granted for a Travellers' site near to their house?

What would your friends and family say if you became partners with a Gypsy, Roma or Traveller person?

Returning to the issue of friendships outside of my immediate family and culture, I have made a select few friends who supported me through the bullying and negativity, and this is something I am still working on now. I grew up with the understanding that mixing with country people is anti-cultural; this has had an impact on my social skills as I always worry that I am being judged by my own. The bullying continued throughout my secondary school time, with comments made daily including '*Is there any need for you to be here, you will only be a housewife anyway?*' Most of the time I was able to ignore these comments, but at other times it would all be too much. It was my determination to succeed which powered me to gain my GCSEs. This drive then led me on to pass college and now I am in my third year at university and am about to begin a master's degree in psychology. My passion is to help others ensure that they have the best start to their life despite any adversity they have faced so far. University has taught me that having experienced the bad does not need to overshadow the good.

Home will always be my favourite place to be, and one of the greatest things about all Gypsy, Roma and Traveller cultures is that family always comes first; always has and always will. I grew up happy and healthy having all my needs and wants met. My mam grew up following tradition, marrying at a young age to my dad, and had me and my brother, Stephen. I grew up living in the family home with a sense of security and being part of a strong family. My mam taught me the ways in which I was to act and develop. However, my parents' divorce happened during my teen years, divorce then being a taboo subject, never spoken of in our traditional community. Being part of a divorced

Gypsy family presented many problems, which other cultures may not experience to such an extent regarding shame and stigma. However, my parents' decision to divorce demonstrated to me that we must do what makes us happy, despite traditions and the scandal it may cause. In the last two years, my mam met her new partner, John, for whom I am thankful. This is because, alongside some family members (not all), he too supports me and my plans. When I travel home to see family, we talk about what I have learnt and look at the next steps in my career. Aside from university life, I also work within a school setting and at my family-run equestrian centre. The equestrian centre prides itself on giving back and being a safe place for the local environment, no matter who you are, and offers opportunities for all ages or abilities to be involved. We have an open-gate policy, and the public are more than welcome to come in. We believe our centre has brought some positive change, especially within an area in which there are not many youth services available. Hopefully, our centre has influenced the ways in which the public see the Gypsy, Roma and Traveller community – they can see us in a positive light: being approachable towards visitors, helping them feel comfortable, and realise that we are just humans like them. However, I doubt Channel 4 will be heading our way soon to make a documentary – *Gypsy Equestrian Centre Helps Youth in Community* – it may not attract enough viewers for their ratings!

Working in a school setting, alongside my university studies, has enabled me to develop my career pathway and has offered many chances in practice. I believed it was time to be open about my ethnicity, although this is still a concern when applying for jobs. The school where I work were accepting of my culture once I spoke openly about it, and I found them willing to know more by having discussions with me. One member of staff stated they were shocked at the discrimination we still experience in the twenty-first century and appeared to be genuinely upset about this.

We live our lives feeling the need to stay within our community to follow our traditions and, in a way, we become sheltered from the world. Taking the decision to go away to uni was a massive decision for me, whereas most young people see such a step as a natural one after secondary school. As I gained confidence away from home, I replied to a university-wide request from Peter Unwin, my co-author, for a student with a Gypsy, Roma, Traveller background who was willing to speak at a conference being held at the University of Winchester. This conference was promoting the 'HE Pledge' (Gypsy, Roma, Traveller, Showmen and Boaters into Higher Education, 2021), which is designed to encourage members of our communities to apply to inclusive universities. At the time of writing, very few universities have signed up to this Pledge, although I was very pleased that the University of Worcester's Student Union signed, hopefully encouraging others to do the same and show some positive signs of embracing students from Gypsy, Roma and Traveller backgrounds. I was the only person to respond to Peter's request and was happy to promote the Pledge, as it is a great initiative. Looking back, I am proud to have taken the risk of accessing higher education and becoming an advocate for the Gypsy, Roma and Traveller community. At the Winchester conference, I was able to speak frankly about my mixed experiences at university and became more aware of my resilience in staying the distance.

Reflective activity

Read the HE Pledge www.bucks.ac.uk/sites/default/files/2021-06/GTRSB% 20into%20HE%20Pledge%20doc.pdf.

Produce your own critique of the Pledge and think of ways in which your organisation, whether a university or a voluntary/statutory agency, could adopt this initiative.

Perhaps you could take some proactive steps to see what needs to be in place within your organisation and challenge any barriers that might be encountered. The Pledge requires attitude rather than money.

I have been very pleased also to hear about initiatives such as the Gypsy, Roma, Traveller Social Work Association (GRTSWA), made up of social workers who are themselves Gypsy, Roma or Travellers. This association is now standing up to fight for rights and better practice within the social work profession. There is a great fear of 'the social' in many of our communities, not just because of historical oppression from governments but because of recent evidence regarding the numbers of our children being removed into state care (Allen and Hamnett, 2022), disability services not being taken up (Unwin et al, 2020) and the mental health crisis not being addressed (Greenfields and Rogers, 2020). I hope that the GRTSWA are successful in changing practices and policies in social work and wider afield in order that Gypsy, Roma and Traveller communities are fully included, rather than in reality being excluded from most policies and practice guides around diversity – 'the excluded within the included'.

On the other hand, it has not been all positive for me in recent years. I have experienced social exclusion within my local area, including being followed around shops, purely based on appearance and the prejudicial belief that '*Gypsies steal*', and I have also been refused service at restaurants. More recently, I had to leave my vacation bar job in a pub because I had served Travellers and made friendly conversation with them. After all, we are a tight-knit community, and we always have family links/friends in common. My boss asked why I was so friendly with Travellers, and once I knew that he was racist, I had no option other than to leave.

Experiences such as these have had a negative impact on my mental health and on my ability to go out in public without the fear of judgement. People do act this way, but not all country people, and a whole community cannot be held accountable for one person's discriminatory actions. During specific times throughout the year events are held such as the Appleby Horse Fair and the Stow Fair in the Cotswolds. During a visit to Stow just before Covid-19 struck, my co-author Peter Unwin was shocked at the racism he witnessed via notices in pubs and shops such as *'Closed for the holidays'*, *'Stock taking – closed all week'*, *'Closed for essential maintenance'*, when really these signs meant *'Gypsies, Roma and Travellers not welcome'*. How is this acceptable?

Reflective activity

Antigypsism has been described as the *'last acceptable form of racism'* (Traveller Movement, 2017) and this racism can be seen to affect the social exclusion of Gypsies, Roma and Travellers, starting at the top with a government determined to dismantle the hard-won Human Rights Act 1998. The passing of the Police, Crime, Sentencing and Courts Act 2022 can be seen as a means to eliminate, not just exclude, whole cultures of Travellers. Please study the provisions of this Act and take a view on whether they conflict with the Human Rights Act 1998, Article 8, which protects the right to a private and family life, which includes your home.

The Police, Crime, Sentencing and Courts Act 2022 allows for the impounding and possible destruction of vehicles (homes), the removal of children into state care and criminalises a nomadic way of life and work that has been part of British culture for centuries. Even the chief police officers did not want this Act made law as they were satisfied that unauthorised encampments could already be dealt with via negotiation and existing civil laws of trespass.

Why then, do you think the Conservative government drew up and passed the above Act?

You might also reflect on how you would feel, if you now live in a flat, bungalow or house, and a law was passed to say that if you continued to live in that type of dwelling, you would be arrested, your home taken away and any children removed into state care?

At the same time, reflect on the recent words of an old and frail Welsh Gypsy woman, who had been taken into care many decades ago and placed in settings outside of her culture (even today there are hardly any Gypsy, Roma or Traveller kinship foster carers). She is now a wife, mother, grandmother and great-grandmother. Upon being asked by her daughter *'What does home mean to you, mam?',* her reply was *'No walls... open countryside... moving with family... the open sky. I only ever wanted to live in a caravan, and I want to die in one.'* Is that so very much to ask?

Gypsy, Roma and Traveller communities and organisations have not been passive in the face of social exclusion and discrimination, but they are relatively small in number. The Traveller Movement (2018) estimate there were approx. 300,000 Gypsies, Roma and Travellers living in the UK but noted that all data relating to Gypsy, Roma and Traveller populations is questionable due largely to under-reporting of ethnicity and services not collecting data appropriately. One example of activism and protest is the 'Traveller Lives Matter' movement, which began in September 2020. This came about due to a pub in my local area refusing entry to Travellers, stating they have been instructed not to let them in. The protest brought wide social media attention around the racism Gypsy, Roma and Traveller people face.

People's perceptions of the Gypsy, Roma and Traveller community are influenced by a variety of factors, including social media, television programmes and influence from others. Programmes over time have presented us in many more negative ways than positive ways. As times has moved on, social media has increasingly influenced people's views. Most recently, lots of videos, especially on TikTok, have been posted which stereotype us from a non-Traveller/Gypsy perspective – usually making a mockery of us and our culture. The old tales about how we are ill-mannered, untrust-worthy and that we steal babies and belongings endure, albeit in different formats. These tales still influence people's perceptions, but I strongly believe you cannot judge someone because of their culture; clearly, many people think otherwise and judge us unmercifully.

Reflective activity

Think of a time you went to a shop recently:

Were you refused entry?

Were you followed by security?

Were you accused?

How do you think it would affect your mental health to be constantly watched and followed by security staff every time you went shopping?

The above exercise is just one example of how other people's views affect us daily. These misconceptions are not recent but have been there over time. From speaking with my mam, she highlighted the fact that segregation was prevalent throughout her childhood, stating, '*It has always been them and us*'. I hope that as times change and awareness grows that people begin to accept us for who we are as a community. I recently saw a picture that showed Tyson Fury, a champion boxer of Gypsy heritage, with the caption '*We all chant Gypsy King, but as soon as we see a caravan, we call the police*'. Seeing that caption shows that people are ignorant towards us and judge us for what they see on various media platforms. Personally, I strongly advocate that people need to see us in the real world and current times. We are just people like everyone else. I would like others to just see us as fellow human beings, and not refer to us as '*Pikeys*' or '*Scum*' – we just want to live our life with the acceptance of others, and not have to be forever excluded.

I also intend to work further with organisations that promote the Gypsy, Roma and Traveller communities' access to higher education, and generally help reduce stigmatisation and labelling, thus improving our mental health, self-esteem and happiness. Having a label has been something I have always had to deal with. I find it difficult at times and it has a negative impact on my mental health as I feel so isolated from others. However, for me, the 'Gypsy' label also makes me who I am, and I am proud.

Being a part of my community is something I would never change, despite the social exclusion and discrimination we face. I genuinely believe that being part of this community has positively shaped me into the person I am today, and I am proud of that. From an early age I was taught life lessons which are still effective now. We are a family-oriented community, and I am thankful for the bond I have with my mam. Our community is caring and has respect for each other. We stand by one another and are there to support each other when needed. We may not know one another and our personal stories; however, we say '*Hello*' to each other, and ask how things are. It could be said that we follow the same old traditions with the intention to live a happy life with our own family and follow our own path. However, I did not strictly conform to those traditions – I wanted an education and wanted to be my own person, with a decent career. This has had an impact on the way others look at me, including those from the same community, but I will not let their judgement disrupt my goals, even if it means being disowned or excluded by some family and friends. Wanting an education now, especially us girls, is more common, and some small businesses have been successfully created by our girls, which is a huge achievement.

After I have achieved my goals in gaining what I can from education, I intend to settle. As stated above, we believe family is of the utmost importance, and I will be bringing my children up with the family involved. However, the option for my children to stay in education will be given and, as encouraged by my mam, I will encourage my children to attend school and to be supported in whatever they decide to do in life. I hope when this time comes that the Gypsy, Roma and Traveller community are accepted in society and the segregation between us and country people, if not gone, is less in evidence. I will inform my children that, despite what others may say, be proud to be who you are! Do not hide it away in fear of others' opinions and you must believe that anything can be achieved.

Writing this chapter has made me reflect on how resilient I have had to be to get to university and have aspirations that bridge cultures. However, it should not be so hard, and I hope that some of the positive developments discussed in this chapter will bring about a future where Gypsy, Roma and Traveller people do not have to jump so many hurdles and suffer ongoing social exclusion. Readers can make a start in bringing about such changes simply by showing interest in our communities, which I would take as a sign of respect, not nosiness. Only when we begin to discuss such issues together can we counter the negative stereotypes that have dogged our families for too long.

Helpful resources to find out more about Gypsy, Roma and Traveller issues

Friends, Families and Travellers: www.gypsy-traveller.org

The Romani Cultural and Arts Company: www.romaniarts.co.uk

Travellers Movement: https://travellermovement.org.uk

Travellers' Times: www.travellerstimes.org.uk

Travelling Ahead: Gypsy, Roma and Traveller Advice and Advocacy Service:

www.travellingahead.org.uk/contact

References

All Ireland Traveller Health Study Team (2010) All Ireland Traveller Health Study. [online] Available at: www.gov.ie/en/publication/b9c48a-all-ireland-traveller-health-study (accessed 8 August 2022).

Allen, D and Hamnett, V (2022) Gypsy, Roma and Traveller Children in Child Welfare Services in England. *The British Journal of Social Work*. https://doi.org/10.1093/bjsw/bcab265

Allen, D and Hulmes, A (2021) Aversive Racism and Child Protection Practice with Gypsy, Roma and Traveller Children and Families. *Seen and Heard*, 31(2). [online] Available at: www.nagalro.com/_userfiles/pages/files/allen_hulmes_aversive_racismjs.pdf (accessed 8 August 2022).

British Association of Social Workers (2022) Social Workers Tell Comic Jimmy Carr to Stand Down from Welsh Show. [online] Available at: www.basw.co.uk/resources/psw-magazine/psw-online/social-workers-tell-comic-jimmy-carr-stand-down-welsh-show (accessed 8 August 2022).

Channel 4 (2022) *60 Days with the Gypsies.* [online] Available at: www.channel4.com/programmes/60-days-with-the-gypsies (accessed 8 August 2022).

Dovidio, J F and Gaertner, S L (eds) (1986) The Aversive Form of Racism. In *Prejudice, Discrimination and Racism* (pp 61–89). San Diego, CA: Academic Press.

Equality Act 2010 [online] Available at: www.legislation.gov.uk/ukpga/2010/15/contents (accessed 8 August 2022).

Greenfields, M and Rogers, C (2020) Hate: 'As Regular as Rain'. A Pilot Research Project into the Psychological Effects of Hate Crime on Gypsy, Traveller and Roma (GTR) Communities. A Report Commissioned by GATE HERTS and Funded by the Ministry of Housing, Communities and Local Government (MHCLG). [online] Available at: https://gateherts.org.uk/wp-content/uploads/2020/12/Rain-Report-201211.pdf (accessed 9 August 2022).

Gypsy, Roma, Traveller, Showmen and Boaters into Higher Education (2021) *Improving Access & Participation in Higher Education for Gypsies, Travellers, Roma, Showmen & Boaters. Take the Pledge.* [online] Available at: www.bucks.ac.uk/sites/default/files/2021-06/GTRSB%20into%20HE%20Pledge%20doc.pdf (accessed 8 August 2022).

Human Rights Act 1998 [online] Available at: www.legislation.gov.uk/ukpga/1998/42/contents (accessed 8 August 2022).

Open Society Foundations (2013) Gypsies, Roma, Travellers: An Animated History. [online] Available at: www.youtube.com/watch?v=Q6wSLfGBVGY (accessed 8 August 2022).

Page, C and McGlinchey, C (2022) Irish Travellers 'Mental Health Crisis' Driven by Discrimination and Deprivation. *BBC News,* 18 April. [online] Available at: www.bbc.co.uk/news/world-europe-61117469 (accessed 8 August 2022).

Plunkett, J (2012) Big Fat Gypsy Weddings 'Has Increased Bullying of Gypsies and Travellers'. *The Guardian,* 16 October. [online] Available at: www.theguardian.com/media/2012/oct/16/big-fat-gypsy-weddings-bullying-travellers (accessed 8 August 2022).

Police, Crime, Sentencing and Courts Act 2022 [online] Available at: www.legislation.gov.uk/ukpga/2022/32/contents/enacted (accessed 8 August 2022).

Traveller Movement (2017) The Last Acceptable Form of Racism? The Pervasive Discrimination and Prejudice Experienced by Gypsy, Roma and Traveller Communities. [online] Available at: https://travellermovement.org.uk/policy-and-publications/the-last-acceptable-form-of-racism (accessed 8 August 2022).

Traveller Movement (2018) Gypsy Roma and Traveller History and Culture. [online] Available at: https://travellermovement.org.uk/gypsy-roma-and-traveller-history-and-culture (accessed 8 August 2022).

Travellers' Times Films (2013) *Gypsies, Roma and Travellers – An Animated History.* Open Society Foundations. [online] Available at: www.youtube.com/watch?v=Q6wSLfGBVGY (accessed 8 August 2022).

Travellers' Times Films (2019) *Roads From the Past.* [online] Available at: www.youtube.com/watch?v=1bhBbMrF8Z0 (accessed 8 August 2022).

Unwin, P, Meakin, B and Jones, A (2020) *The Missing Voices of Disabled People in Gypsy, Roma and Traveller Communities.* [online] Available at: www.drilluk.org.uk/wp-content/uploads/2020/12/Missing-Voices-FINAL-report.pdf (accessed 8 August 2022).

Mel Hughes

Chapter objectives

This chapter will help readers:

»   understand how you can challenge social exclusion and stigma and foster social inclusion;

»   identify different types and approaches to activism;

»   seek inspiration from other activists;

»   consider the challenges involved in taking action and how to overcome them;

»   use reflective exercises to identify your own approach to becoming a social activist.

In this chapter we explore our role as social activists and share ideas on how we can all play our part in challenging social exclusion and fostering social inclusion. We will explore what social activism is, how to become a social activist and how to overcome the challenges involved.

Are you an activist?

Before we start, it would be useful for you to give some thought to your confidence as a social activist. Do you feel confident using your voice or your platform to influence change and to hold people in power to account?

How confident are you that you can:

»   understand the impact of social exclusion on individuals;

»   recognise your own assumptions and beliefs and challenge these;

»   identify strategies to successfully challenge social exclusion and foster social inclusion;

»   become an ally to others to help challenge social exclusion and foster social inclusion;

»   challenge stigma and raise awareness among family and friends;

> » speak up in class about an area of social exclusion and stigma;
>
> » challenge stigma and raise awareness among work/placement colleagues;
>
> » hold people in positions of authority to account about social exclusion and social injustices;
>
> » support or start a campaign/protest/boycott/petition to challenge social exclusion and foster social inclusion.
>
> **Are there some areas you are more or less confident in?**
>
> **If so, are you able to reflect on why this might be?**

Becoming a social activist

Becoming a social activist involves finding your voice and knowing how to use your platform to achieve change. It involves focusing on what you are passionate about and developing an understanding of how you can challenge effectively.

Concepts of citizenship and participation

The *Oxford English Dictionary* defines social activism as '*the activity of working together to achieve political or social change, especially as a member of an organization with particular aims*'. Brenman and Sanchez (2014) explain that the social part refers not only to society but also to how social activism can create opportunities for participation. Underpinning social activism is the concept of citizenship and the power we have as individuals to participate as full and active members of our society. This can hold different meanings for different people and communities. In its broadest sense, citizenship can refer to a person's legal and cultural status within a society and the role they play within it (Ponce and Rowe, 2018). Some writers have identified that these roles, responsibilities and opportunities, however, are based on social norms and, as such, benefit some groups more than others (Atterbury and Rowe, 2017; Beresford, 2019). Those most affected by health, social and economic inequalities often have the least opportunity to inform and shape the societal structures, policies and practices that affect them. Not being able to fully participate leads to further exclusion and marginalisation as their views and experiences are not heard or understood by those in positions of authority.

A helpful concept in relation to this book and chapter is *active citizenship*, which typically refers to citizens who are proactive in engaging in activism and promoting participation to create a more inclusive and fair society for all. Wood (2009) conducted a research study exploring concepts of active citizenship with young people. The concepts of active citizenship that the young people deemed to be most important were '*rights*', '*responsibilities*', '*care for others*', '*control*', '*making decisions*' and '*respect*' (Wood, 2009). Specific conditions, however, are required to make this possible. Active citizenship and participation and, as a result, social inclusion, require those of us in positions of power and influence to create spaces and opportunities for everyone to participate.

A theoretical view

Jürgen Habermas, a German sociologist, drew on the concepts of *lifeworld* and *system world* to explain the imbalance of power between people in charge and the rest of society. He explains how those in the system world (governments, policy makers, public organisations) are motivated by different priorities than those situated in the lifeworld. The system world is often driven by structures, economics and processes, whereas the lifeworld is more about lived experiences, social relationships and the realities of everyday life. Habermas argued that shared spaces need to be created to bring people together to communicate, gain knowledge and find common ground (Habermas, 1987, 1991). The American philosopher and feminist Nancy Fraser (1990) argued that everyone has the right to be an active citizen and inform decisions which affect them but that specific social arrangements need to be developed to ensure that everyone can participate as equal peers in public life. As social activists, we can participate in and influence public life based on lifeworld priorities and help create spaces and opportunities for everyone's voices to be heard.

Barriers to becoming a social activist

There are barriers to speaking out and using our voice and our platform. These can often be explained by the previous discussion on citizenship and not feeling that we have the power or authority to speak out. If we work for an organisation; or live in a country where there are consequences for challenging authority, we may feel that it is not safe to do so. Not speaking out can also be due to apathy and a feeling that we won't make a difference or that there is no point. It is common to question if it is our fight; to feel that we don't know enough; to worry what other people might think, or that there are other people who can do this better than we can. Not doing anything, however, or waiting for someone else to do something maintains the status quo and prevents change from happening. As the definitions of social activism, citizenship and participation suggest, activism involves working together with others to achieve change. The more of us involved, the bigger the impact.

So, what can you do?

Finding inspiration

There are many activists that we can take inspiration from. The following are quotes that can guide us as we seek to develop ways to advance social justice and foster social inclusion.

Which of these quotes are you drawn to?

You may never know what results come of your actions, but if you do nothing, there will be no results.

Mahatma Gandhi

We realise the importance of our voices only when we are silenced.

Malala Yousafzai

As my sufferings mounted, I soon realised that there were two ways in which I could respond to my situation – either to react with bitterness or seek to transform the suffering into a creative force. I decided to follow the latter course.

Martin Luther King Jr

Education is the most powerful weapon which you can use to change the world.

Nelson Mandela

Activism is the rent I pay for living on this planet.

Alice Walker

If not us, then who? If not now, then when?

John Lewis, Freedom Rider

Are there other quotes or inspiring activists that you would add? Who inspires you to take action?

> *Examples of social activism*
>
> #MeToo and Black Lives Matter are specific examples of hugely impactful social activism in recent years. There are others too. In 2019, *The Big Issue* compiled a list of their Top 100 changemakers: www.bigissue.com/news/activism/the-big-issues-top-100-changemakers-2019-campaigns-and-campaigners
>
> **What is it about these examples that led them to be so successful?**
>
> **What can we learn from them?**

Becoming a social activist involves:

» recognising and harnessing the power and influence you have;

» learning that saying something is better than saying nothing;

» learning that small acts can lead to big change;

» learning that you don't need to know everything; you just need to know it's not right;

» reflecting on your own role and responsibilities.

Starting with yourself

When frustrated about the injustices around us, it can be tempting to focus on what you believe everyone else needs to do. While challenging social exclusion requires a community and a society response, we need to start with ourselves. We all make assumptions and have preconceived ideas about the world around us. We are all a product of our upbringing and our environment. To be a social activist we need to reflect and challenge any taken-for-granted norms and assumptions we may have. An important first step in activism involves engaging in a process of reflecting on our beliefs and educating ourselves about the reality of living and lived experiences for those around us. What are your beliefs? What are these based on and where do they come from? How influenced are you by the views of the media or others around you? How accurate are they? What is the reality for specific groups and communities experiencing social exclusion in the UK? How, as a society, have we created and why do we maintain this inequality and inequity? Challenging social exclusion involves you reflecting on how you engage with and view groups within our society and how you reinforce or challenge stigma and social exclusion.

> ## Activity
>
> The **RED** acronym can help guide this process.
>
> **R**: Reflect and challenge your own beliefs and attitudes.
>
> **E**: Educate yourself on the realties and the evidence for people's social exclusion and what needs to happen for this to improve.
>
> **D**: Do something to challenge this and to foster social inclusion.

Doing something

Challenging social exclusion and stigma will often involve engaging in a range of types and approaches to activism. The question is often where to start. The best way is to find something that you are passionate about. Your passion to challenge a particular type of social exclusion and stigma could be because it's personal; that it affects you, your family and friends; that you have observed the impact on those around you (at home, in your community or workplace, on the TV and in social media). It could be that through education, you are aware of the impact of social exclusion and feel strongly that something needs to change. It might not be your lived experience, but you want to be an ally and be part of the solution. Whatever your motivation, it involves 'doing something'.

With so many types and approaches to activism, part of becoming an activist involves finding what works for you and what has the most impact. Here are ten ways to be an activist for inspiration.

Ten ways to be an activist

1. Start a conversation.

2. Volunteer.

3. Amplify seldom-heard voices.

4. Support an existing campaign.

5. Become politically engaged.

6. Join or start a local community group.

7. Share or create materials and resources.

8. Donate or fundraise.

9. Harness social media.

10. Engage in slow activism.

These are further explored here

1. Start a conversation

Some forms of activism can feel quite daunting. Starting a conversation may feel small but can be powerful in raising awareness, challenging misinformation or misconceptions and in educating yourself. You can start with friends and family. A conversation should be a dialogue; a two-way process which involves listening and sharing. Be curious, show interest, seek to understand the other person's viewpoint and share your own thoughts in an open and honest way. Bear in mind that *attack* is often met with *defence*. Your aim is not to tell someone they are wrong or convert them to your viewpoint. Starting conversations should come from a place of openness and curiosity. Have conversations with people who share your view and those who don't.

2. Volunteer

Doing something can take many forms but volunteering online or in person for a community organisation can have significant impact. This can include a range of opportunities and roles including direct action (volunteering for a campaign) and direct involvement (volunteering with socially excluded groups). For opportunities in your area, you can contact your local volunteer centre (www.ncvo.org.uk/ncvo-volunteer ing/find-a-volunteer-centre) or type 'volunteer opportunities' into a search engine. Many national charities have a *Volunteer* or *How can I get involved?* section on their website.

3. Amplify seldom-heard voices

Many people who experience social exclusion and stigma can feel powerless and unheard. Creating an opportunity for people to share their stories, as we have in this book, can be a powerful way of triggering humanised and compassionate responses which lead to action. This involves you engaging and connecting with people who are directly affected. Stories don't only focus on what happened to someone. They provide a way for someone to reclaim their narrative, challenge misconceptions and contribute their expertise on what needs to change. Amplifying seldom-heard voices can shift the power balance. Sharing stories can take many forms (written stories, podcasts, blogs, TV, film, social media, verbal conversations). If you have experienced social exclusion and stigma, give thought to how you can speak out and share your story and expertise. For all of us, give thought to how you can share living and lived experience stories and amplify these voices. For example, can you share specific chapters from this book?

4. Support an existing campaign

Collective action can be far more powerful than a single voice. Depending on your area of interest, there are likely to be people who share your views and groups and organisations already working to challenge this social exclusion and stigma. Many of the big charities run campaigns to change government policy or legislation. You can access these links for examples and can seek out charities working in areas that you are passionate about to see what they are doing and how you can be involved.

www.crisis.org.uk/get-involved/campaign/campaign-successes

www.stonewall.org.uk/campaign-with-us

www.mentalhealth.org.uk/our-work/campaigns

www.ageuk.org.uk/our-impact/campaigning

5. Become politically engaged

Becoming politically engaged can take a number of forms, including choosing to vote in an election; discussing politics with others; contacting an elected official (local councillor or member of parliament); responding to a government consultation; joining and supporting a political party; standing for election; taking part in a demonstration or protest; signing a petition; joining a union; or supporting a national or local campaign calling for policy or legal change or reform. Becoming politically engaged can be daunting if you have not experienced it before. Councils and governments, however, are elected to represent local people. A requirement of their role is to understand and represent the views and priorities of local people and constituents. If we don't make our views known or advocate for seldom-heard groups, they will not be able to represent us. You can find out who your local MP is and how to contact them here: www.parliament.uk/get-involved/contact-an-mp-or-lord/contact-your-mp. If you are interested in seeing how your local MP has represented you to date, you can see a summary of how they have voted here: www.theyworkforyou.com

6. Join or start a local community group

Find out if there are already people who share your views and are doing something in your local area or online. Can you join them? Are there people directly affected by social exclusion who are seeking to achieve change? Can you support them and be an ally? If there is nothing in your area, you could be the one to start a group. You could arrange a meeting with people to share ideas and gauge interest. Your group could have a social and networking focus; it could be a campaign group; it could be a space to share information and peer support; it could be linked to a particular community or project, such as a group within a school, university or workplace. Start small and let people know that you exist. If you find a group from another area or country with a similar goal, you can contact them so you can learn from them and seek guidance and support. You don't need to reinvent the wheel.

7. Share or create materials and resources

Often social activism is prompted by a gap or a need that you have identified yourself. It may be that you were looking for information or resources on a particular topic or area of social exclusion or stigma. If you find that these resources don't exist or you find them and think that others might find them helpful too, you can create or share them. This could be in the form of a fact sheet, leaflet, social media page or post. It could be a list of local resources or support services; facts and figures; useful contacts or tips and ideas. Give thought to what would be most helpful, who you can involve, how you can fact check what you have included and how you can ensure it reaches the people who need it most.

8. Donate or fundraise

Existing campaigns, organisations and support groups will often appreciate your financial support, whether a one-off or a regular donation. If you are able to, make a donation or find out how you can fundraise for them. Always do his through reputable organisations so you know that your donation will be used effectively and for the greatest impact.

9. Harness social media

Social media can feel a bit like the Wild West sometimes due to the lack of regulation and the prevalence of online trolling. It has been shown, however, to be a force for good in connecting people to global and local communities and networks and for sharing resources and support. The #MeToo and Black Lives Matter campaigns had the global impact they did because of social media. As a social activist, you can harness social media by using it to find and link to online communities and 'liking' and 'following' prominent activists and campaigners that you support.

10. Engage in slow activism

In 2014, the activist Sarah Corbett presented a TED talk on why activism needs introverts. An introvert herself, Corbett comments on how activism can often focus on the urgent need to take action now. While not disagreeing, she presents three types of slow activism which can have a significant impact and are needed if we are to achieve and sustain meaningful change. *Quiet activism* involves, for example, crafting sessions as a way of bringing introverts into activism and developing deeper thoughtful conversations. *Intimate activism* involves listening to people with different views to your own and building bridges, while *intriguing activism* involves engaging people in non-confrontational ways, for example, through street art or wearing ribbons or badges as a conversation starter. For inspiration and ideas, you can access the full talk here: www.ted.com/talks/sarah_corbett_activism_needs_introverts

Case studies

In the remainder of this chapter, we share four case studies written by social work students on what they are doing to challenge social exclusion, how they are using their voice and platform and why.

The students featured are part of a BA (Hons) social work cohort undertaking a second-year unit on social justice and social work. As part of the unit, students were required to identify an area of social injustice to explore, and then to take action to advance social justice in this area. They engaged in activism to raise awareness, educate, campaign, challenge, support and to start conversations. Their activism covered a whole range of issues relating to LGBT+, looked after children, climate change, older age and isolation, hidden disabilities, homelessness, refugees and many more. Four of the students share their activism here as examples of finding their voice and using their platform to challenge social exclusion and stigma and to promote social inclusion. Case study 5 has been left blank for you to complete.

Case study 1 Challenging the access gap to higher education, Jasmine Thomson

What: I believe everyone should have a right to further their education. It should not be unachievable because of where you were born. At school I was told repeatedly *'you won't be able to do that'*. I am a single parent, living in a low socio-economic area and if this disparity continues it could negatively impact my son's future.

Why: People from low socio-economic backgrounds are less likely to attend university with the disparity increasing when looking at many ethnic minority groups. In England, the average participation rate in higher education by age 19 is 39.70 per cent; when looking at Weymouth and Portland in Dorset, where I live, the average participation rate by 19 is 27.50 per cent (DfE, 2019). Weymouth and Portland is an area with high levels of deprivation. The government is looking to pass higher education policy and reform which will prevent people with low grades from getting student loans. Students from lower socio-economic backgrounds are less likely to achieve the same grades as peers in less deprived areas. This will disproportionately affect mature and younger applicants to university from lower socio-economic backgrounds.

How: I challenged this by writing to my MP with my concerns about the new policy and by filling out the online higher education policy statement and reform consultation. I arranged a talk at the sixth form I attended and spoke to students about different routes into university, as I am now studying at university as a mature student. My Conservative MP responded to say he shared my concerns about this policy and forwarded my email on to the Minister of State for Universities and Higher Education. I received positive feedback from the students I spoke to at the sixth form for informing them of alternative perspectives and routes into higher education that they hadn't been aware of.

I learnt it is hard to challenge new government policies. Consultation forms are complex, and your MP can take weeks to respond. Bullet pointing my concerns helped my MP and the Minister of State to respond to each one. My advice is: get someone to proofread before you press send to make sure you have been clear, concise and not emotional.

Case study 2 Bin liners are not suitcases, Niamh Howlett

What: I had regular contact with social workers as my family had fostered since I was young. This is what ultimately inspired my passion to become a social worker. I saw the effects that the 'little' things had on a child, including the use of bin liners to move their belongings between homes. Even as a child I knew this was wrong so when the opportunity arose to raise awareness, I jumped at the chance.

Why: In 2021, the National Youth Advocacy Service reported that four in five looked after children said their belongings had been moved in binbags when they moved placements during their time in care (Downie and Twomey, 2022). Some children I work with feel so unimportant and small and are living through difficult situations they shouldn't have to. I feel it is vital to make them feel heard and valued but how can we if we are using bin liners to transport their belongings? From conversations I had with foster carers, there is a clear impact on young people's mental health when bin liners are used to move belongings yet there is very little awareness of the issue and minimal research showing the impact. Sometimes it feels impossible to raise awareness or make a change.

How: I chose to work with the Buddy Bag Foundation, who provide bags with toiletries and toys in them to children in care or who are fleeing domestic violence situations (Buddy Bag Foundation, 2021). They rely on volunteers to make and send in toiletry and sanitary product bags, so I and other family members made bags using recycled material. I put out a post on my Facebook page to explain what I was doing and why.

Through this experience I learnt doing something is better than nothing. I hope by putting it out there I have raised awareness of the issue and even if one person thinks more about it or speaks with a friend in the future, then I feel I have made a positive impact and at least started the conversation to initiate future change.

Case study 3 Starting the conversation, Lee Forde

What: Before starting the social work course, I worked in a social and emotional mental health (SEMH) primary school. This, paired with having a young daughter, really highlighted the importance of support for young people. My research and activism are based around 'precocious puberty', when puberty begins before age eight in girls, and the effects this can have on their mental health.

Why: Young people can experience social exclusion and stigma due to the lack of support and guidance for girls beginning to menstruate early or being 'out of step' with their peers. This leaves many girls living in a constant state of anxiety from a very young age. This impact is an issue due to the problems and difficulties that this experience can result in later in their lives. For example, the earlier puberty is reached by a young girl, the higher the chance of depression, anxiety, use of substances and smoking, as well as unwanted teenage pregnancy. There is also an issue with the stigma surrounding menstruation, with people still to this day thinking that it is 'disgusting' or 'dirty' and the negative effects this feeling of shame has on them.

How: I was able to use my voice to work with primary schools and businesses selling sanitary products to begin to raise awareness around the subject. Working to create easily accessible information and guidance for young girls throughout their time at primary school, while providing sanitary products and four sanitary bins to a primary school in Essex.

This project has had a life-changing effect on me. It has shown me how it really doesn't take much to use your voice and try to help others. My advice to others would be to try not to judge what you are doing by how big the result is. Just starting to have the conversation is a huge step in the right direction.

Case study 4 We are all human, Venus Ip

What: I am a second-year social work student at Bournemouth University. I moved to the UK from Hong Kong eight months ago. Many immigrants, whether by choice or forced to move from another country, often experience a difficult process to adapt to a new, unfamiliar environment.

Why: Berry (2003) described the process of adaptation of an individual, immigrants, refugees or asylum seekers as acculturation. In Berry's acculturation theory, he suggested four key outcomes of the acculturation process: segregation; integration; assimilation; marginalisation. Migrated individuals going through acculturation risk facing social exclusion; in other words, being marginalised from the new society they have moved to. The consequences of being socially excluded are the origin of many social issues in host societies. According to Chung and Bemak (2012), marginalised individuals have been shown to have the highest levels of risk for poverty, substance misuse, family conflicts and mental health conditions.

How: To take action to address this, I reached out to immigrants online through an online chat forum for migrants, refugees and asylum seekers; and in person by speaking with international students and people at taxi ranks, takeaways and a hotel which housed asylum seekers. I set up a page on Facebook called Humans of Bournemouth. It is a visual project capturing the voices of those who left their countries, have chosen to build a new life here in Bournemouth and call this place their home. Humans of Bournemouth (HOB) is a platform for those who started a new life here to tell their story. Each immigrant has their own unique story to tell. The aim of HOB is to explore who they are, why they came and how they started a new life in Bournemouth. To celebrate the uniqueness of each lived experience.

HOB aims to benefit: 1. The person who shared their immigration story; to explore their social and cultural identity and foster a sense of belonging. 2. The immigrant community; to understand that they are not alone from reading others' lived experiences of acculturation. 3. The 'locals' with the dominant culture; to have more understanding of the challenges and the realities of the process of integration to remove labels, stereotypes and hatred. People are so much more than just a label. I am hoping that by naming the project *Humans of Bournemouth*, other people can see that as well.

Case study 5 has been left blank for you to complete

What is an area of social exclusion you are keen to challenge?

Why is this important?

How can you take action or have you taken action?

What impact will this have/has this had?

References

Atterbury, K and Row, M (2017) Citizenship, Community Mental Health, and the Common Good. *Behavioral Sciences & the Law*, 35(1–2).

Beresford, P (2019) Public Participation in Health and Social Care: Exploring the Co-production of Knowledge. *Frontiers in Sociology*, 3: 41.

Berry, J W (2003) Conceptual Approaches to Acculturation. In Chun, K M, Organista, P B and Marín, G (eds) *Acculturation: Advances in Theory, Measurement, and Applied Research* (pp 17–37). Washington, DC: American Psychological Association.

Big Issue (2019) *The Big Issue*'s Top 100 Changemakers 2019: Campaigns and Campaigners. [online] Available at: www.bigissue.com/news/activism/the-big-issues-top-100-changemakers-2019-campaigns-and-campaigners (accessed 8 August 2022).

Brenman, M and Sanchez, T W (2014) Social Activism. In Michalos, A C (eds) *Encyclopedia of Quality of Life and Well-Being Research* (pp 6012–17). Dordrecht: Springer.

Buddy Bag Foundation (2021) Make a Difference to a Child in Emergency Care. [online] Available at: https://buddybagfoundation.co.uk (accessed 8 August 2022).

Chung, R C and Bemak, F P (2012) *Social Justice Counselling: The Next Steps Beyond Multiculturalism*. Thousand Oaks, CA: Sage.

Corbett, S (2014) Activism Needs Introverts. TED talk. [online] Available at: www.ted.com/talks/sarah_corbett_activism_needs_introverts (accessed 8 August 2022).

Department for Education (DfE) (2019) Participation Rates in Higher Education: 2006 to 2018. London: Department for Education. [online] Available at: www.gov.uk/government/statistics/participation-rates-in-higher-education-2006-to-2018 (accessed 8 August 2022).

Downie, J and Twomey, B (2022) *My Things Matter Report: Support and Respect Care-Experienced Children and Their Belongings When They Move*. Birkenhead: National Youth Advocacy Service.

Fraser, N (1990) Rethinking the Public Sphere: A Contribution to the Critique of Actually Existing Democracy. *Social Text*, 25/26: 56–80.

Habermas, J (1987) *The Theory of Communicative Action, Vol. 2: Lifeworld and System: A Critique of Functionalist Reason*. Boston, MA: Beacon Press.

Habermas, J (1991) *The Structural Transformation of the Public Sphere: An Inquiry into a Category of Bourgeois Society*. Cambridge, MA: MIT Press, pp 175–7.

National Youth Advocacy Service (2022) My Things Matter. [online] Available at: www.nyas.net/news-and-campaigns/campaigns/current-campaigns/my-things-matter (accessed 8 August 2022).

Ponce, A.N and Rowe, M (2018) Citizenship and Community Mental Health Care. *Americal Journal of Community Psychology*, 11 January. https://onlinelibrary.wiley.com/doi/10.1002/ajcp.12218.

Wood, J J (2009) *Young People and Active Citizenship: An Investigation*. PhD thesis, De Montfort University. [online] Available at: https://dora.dmu.ac.uk/bitstream/handle/2086/3234/Jason%20Wood%20-%20Thesis%20-%20e-version.pdf?sequence=1 (accessed 8 August 2022).

Conclusion

Mel Hughes

Chapter objectives

This chapter will help readers:

» reflect on the book's aims and what their learning from it might be;

» consider some key themes from the different chapters and the impact (positive and negative) of these;

» recognise that each experience in this book is unique to the person who shared it and how their story can be used to trigger further exploration;

» consider their next steps in challenging social exclusion in the UK.

Throughout this book we have shared many examples of stigma and social exclusion and the often very difficult life experiences which have led to this. By focusing on specific living and lived experiences we have sought to highlight the impact of social exclusion on people's lives. Each story is unique but there are shared themes and experiences. The chapter contributors have given us a glimpse into their lives and their experiences of social exclusion. They have shared their thoughts on why this happens; the impact this has had and continues to have on their lives; and how they have sought to overcome these barriers. A common theme for the contributors in this book is that they are often excluded by others by the nature of judgements and assumptions being made about them and systems which fail to understand or reflect their needs. Amplifying their voices can help challenge the stigma around a lived experience or a label. Sharing stories can enable you as the reader to put yourself in their shoes. The aim of the book has been to enhance your insight and understanding of a person's situation and to generate more humanised and compassionate responses. As highlighted in Chapter 11, 'Becoming an activist', the ultimate goal is for you to now act on these insights to advance social inclusion and make a difference to the lives of people who are socially excluded and stigmatised.

Reflective activity

» As you were reading through each of the narratives and lived experiences in this book, were there any themes or patterns that you noticed?

> » Can you make a list of some of the common factors or features?
>
> » On completion of your list, are you able to reflect on why these were common factors or features?

Themes

While every experience outlined in this book is unique, there were several recurring factors and features for those experiencing social exclusion. These include disadvantage, concepts of deserving and undeserving, discrimination, stigma including internalised stigma, and limited social capital. Many of these are linked to common experiences including adverse childhood experiences, domestic violence, poor mental health, substance use and poverty, which featured in many of the chapters. These can all be considered as both causes and consequences of social exclusion.

Disadvantage

The lived experience narratives throughout this book demonstrated multiple disadvantages created for people who are socially excluded, often with each aspect compounding another. The narratives demonstrate how people are often repeatedly prevented access to opportunities afforded to others. Myka, Shannon, Phil and Christine, for example, all identified the impact of adverse childhood experiences (ACEs), the consequences of which disrupted their schooling; affected how they formed relationships, their mental health and self-esteem; and affected how they were viewed and judged by others. This early disadvantage impacted decisions they made and opportunities they were afforded later in life. Lisa-Marie spoke of a positive and loving childhood but one that was marred by the judgements and actions of others outside of her community. Ahed describes a life of relative privilege in Syria. She talks of having a flat, a good job, an education. This, however, was all taken away from her when war broke out in her country, removing even the most limited access to basics such as food, shelter and safety. Disadvantage for the book contributors and more generally for people experiencing social exclusion can come in many forms with many causes. The consequences, however, are often very similar. They put people at a disadvantage when seeking to access opportunities often taken for granted by others.

Deserving and undeserving

In Chapter 1: 'Understanding social exclusion', Sally Lee discusses the prevailing concept of categorising people as *deserving and undeserving*. This concept was developed from the poor laws in the 1600s where decisions were made based on who was most deserving or undeserving of relief. Recipients were grouped in terms of those who were not to blame for their circumstances, for example widows or orphans, and those who were viewed as having brought their circumstances upon themselves, for example single mothers or substance users. The latter were seen as less deserving of support and resources. The concept of deserving and undeserving was reflected in many of the lived experiences described in this book, even now several centuries later. Myka, for example, describes the experience of being a mother in prison and how she was seen as undeserving of care, compassion and dignity, and denied the right to access maternity services in the same way as other pregnant women. She described this as losing her rights as a mother due to being sentenced. Legislation and government policy afforded Myka the right to good-quality maternity and health care while in prison but limited resources (itself a policy decision) and the attitudes of those she encountered prevented this from being the case. Samantha discusses the legacy of the 1980s HIV/AIDS public health campaigns that stigmatised and attributed blame to specific communities (*'Don't Die of Ignorance'*). Jay reflects on the views expressed regarding the trans community and transitioning being seen as a lifestyle choice. These views, however, fail to recognise the impact of their lived experiences, the complex reasons why someone is socially excluded and how this is sustained through the actions of others.

Discrimination

Discrimination was explored in Chapter 1 and features throughout the lived experience narratives. It refers to the unfair, unequal or prejudicial treatment towards individuals and groups. All of the contributors provide evidence of being treated unfairly as a result of a label or assumption about who they are. Samantha talks about her HIV status being the basis of decisions about her even though her undetectable viral load meant there is no actual risk to others. Shannon discusses how she was unable to play freely or visit friends' houses because she was the *'druggies' child'*. Jay provides an example of being discriminated against by a sports team only when they became aware that he was transgender. Lisa-Marie and Phil both share examples of direct discrimination in the workplace as a result of their culture or their history. All of these examples show the impact of people's attitudes on the opportunities afforded to people who are labelled and socially excluded. These labels are often attributed based on misconceptions or social norms and expectations regarding how someone should behave or conform.

Stigma and internalised stigma

In Chapter 2: 'Understanding stigma', Margarete Parrish discusses the different concepts of stigma in relation to society's expectations. The experience of stigma and being labelled was evident in all of the lived experience chapters. Ahed, for example, talks about how some British people think that all refugees are poor homeless people who come from camps and tents looking to get money and live a better life depending on the benefits that they get from the government. She challenges this misconception. The example itself though feeds into the narrative of deserving and undeserving and how people are labelled according to whether they are seen as deserving of opportunities. Margarete explains the internal and external attributions when discussing stigma. More compassionate responses tend to be present when causes are thought to be outside of a person's control. Even where this is the case, for example, fleeing a war; being in care as a result of parental actions; being transgender or from a particular cultural group such as Romany Gypsy, the lived experiences shared in this book show that this is often accompanied by labels which still seek to attribute blame to the individual and a narrative that suggests they are underserving of opportunities. Lisa-Marie articulates this powerfully when referring to assumptions that people from her community, including her, are thieves or mistreat animals; huge generalisations which impact her life daily.

In Chapter 2, Margarete also explains how stigma relates to a sense of shame and being flawed rather than doing something wrong. This sense of self and a feeling of being flawed was reflected in many of the chapters. It is a concept, however, that is largely constructed by the expectations of wider society and how people and communities are viewed by others. Samantha, in particular, talks about internalised stigma. She negatively labelled herself. Myka talks about questioning whether she had a right to be a mother; Christine talks about blaming herself for her husband's violent and controlling behaviour and describes feeling that she wasn't 'good enough'. Samantha talks about feeling 'dirty' and not wanting to look at herself; Phil talks about dehumanising terms used to describe substance users such as *scumbag, dirty, loser* and *druggie*. These are all actions which sustain the social exclusion of whole communities and groups of people. The word 'dirty' features multiple times throughout the book and across chapters. Its dictionary definition refers to being marked or unclean but also defines '*dirty*' in relation to character such as dirty dealings and being dishonest or dishonourable. This concept reflects Margarete's explanation of stigma being closely linked to feelings of being flawed or having a flawed identity. Not only does society significantly limit the opportunities available to people who are socially excluded; these are compounded by the attitudes of others. For a number of contributors, this was internalised and led to a negative sense of self that further compounded social exclusion. Both Jay and Lisa-Marie talk of the need to embrace their identity and to challenge negative portrayals and misconceptions.

Limited social capital

All of the contributors have experienced success in being able to break down barriers and foster social inclusion. This has not been without its challenges. In Chapter 1, Sally Lee explores access to social capital which enables individuals, communities and societies to participate in networks, norms and social trust that can lead to mutual benefit. Sally explains how social capital includes economic wealth but also the advantages of social networks, cultural capital, including experience of culture, arts and education, and symbolic capital such as status, respect and reputation. Social capital was lacking for all of our contributors, often from an early age. Shannon, Phil and Myka, for example, discuss experiences including neglect, abuse and early exposure to parental alcohol and substance use and mental ill health, which prevented learning, development and opportunities experienced by their peers. The impact of disrupted parenting on their own lives significantly restricted the opportunities afforded to them by others. This is then exacerbated when not having the same opportunities to develop networks, experiences, status or a positive reputation outside of the family home, for example, when school, friendships, wider family relationships and work are also affected. All of the contributors identify ways they have sought to overcome these barriers.

What helps promote social inclusion?

By asking people to share their insights and expertise, we have been able to harness the expertise of people who have experienced and are experiencing social exclusion. This provides us with knowledge and insight of what works to challenge stigma and social exclusion and promote social inclusion. There were a number of positive themes throughout the book regarding what helps.

Embracing your identity and reclaiming the narrative

Lisa-Marie and Jay, in particular, identify a process where they had learnt to embrace their identity and reclaim their narrative. This approach had led many of the book contributors to create and accept opportunities to educate others about their community or lived experience and to challenge misconceptions. Most of the contributors have gravitated to volunteer and work roles where they can draw on their lived experience expertise and where they feel they can be themselves. There is a role for all of us in celebrating lived experience expertise and embracing and accepting who people are. What can you do today to celebrate your own or someone's identity and lived experience expertise?

Finding a community

For most of our contributors, finding a community was key in navigating social exclusion and mitigating against the negative impact of this. Myka and Samantha talk about the acceptance and safety of being around people who accept you for who you are. Jay and Phil talk about the collective knowledge and support you can access by being part of a community of people with a shared history or experience. These are often benefits not afforded to them outside of their community, a situation that we have the power to influence by creating and contributing to a more inclusive and accepting society. What can you do today to create a more inclusive society?

Trusting relationships and going the extra mile

A number of contributors describe turning points in their lives which were as a result of their own incredible resilience and determination but also supported by meeting someone who looked beyond the label. Myka talks about her son's social worker who showed her compassion and understanding while ensuring her son was protected; and the drug and alcohol worker who had belief and faith in her and told her she would walk beside her on the long road of recovery. For Shannon, it was a drama and art therapist: *'Now this lady, I can honestly say... saved my life.'* This person saw beyond the label and Shannon felt she could be her true self. Most importantly, Myka and Shannon describe feeling a connection and a level of trust in that person and the knowledge that they would be supported. What can you do today to show that a person is seen and to start the slow process of building and earning a person's trust?

Seemingly small acts of kindness

Finally, a striking example in the book and one which feels fitting to end on is the power and impact of seemingly small acts of kindness. Ahed describes the actions of a person from the Red Cross who was the first person she met on arrival in the UK.

She welcomed me with a lovely smile on her face, a bunch of flowers and some fruits. This was so important to me personally as I will not forget that moment and that nice smile on her wonderful face. She gave me the impression that we were welcome in her country, and at that moment I felt relieved and forgot about the whole lot of worries which were in my head. I had the feeling of safety, and I was excited to start a new life in the UK.

This is a powerful example of how a seemingly small act of kindness can have a huge impact on a person's life and in breaking down barriers which create and sustain social exclusion. What will you do today to show kindness to others?

Index